Down at the Santa Fe Depot

Down at the
Santa Fe Depot

20 Fresno Poets

edited by

David Kherdian and James Baloian

The Giligia Press ı Fresno

To Philip Levine

ACKNOWLEDGMENTS

JAMES BALOIAN. "Love Poem" (we slept in the grass) first appeared in New American and Canadian Poetry. "The Indians" was first published by the Red Cedar Review. "The Train" first appeared in Road Apple Review.

WILLIAM CHILDRESS. "The Warlock" and "Vampire" first appeared in Poet Lore. "The Addict" first appeared in Poetry, 1965, copyright 1965 by The Modern Poetry Association. Reprinted with permission of the author and of the editor of Poetry.

GLOVER DAVIS. "The Giant" first appeared in Poetry, 1969, copyright 1969 by The Modern Poetry Association. Reprinted with permission of the author and of the editor of Poetry. "From the Dark Room" was first published in The Southern Review.

PETER EVERWINE. "Living By Water" first appeared in Transpacific. "Perhaps It's As You Say" first appeared in Iowa Review.

ROBERT L. JONES. "Something Else Begins" first appeared in the North American Review, copyright 1968 by the University of Northern Iowa.

DAVID KHERDIAN. "Moving Along Douglas Avenue" and "Howie and Me" first appeared in Cafe Solo.

PHILIP LEVINE. "Renaming the Kings" first appeared in Jeopardy. "Saturday Sweeping" first appeared in Kayak. "Red Dust" first appeared in Iowa Review. "They Feed They Lion" originally appeared in Kayak. "The Angels of Detroit" first appeared in the Unicorn Journal.

LARRY LEVIS. "Mountains" first appeared in Syracuse Poems, 1963-1969, edited by George P. Elliott, published and copyright by Syracuse University Press, 1969. "Bat Angels" first appeared in Nickel Review. "Fish" was published in Intro # 2, edited by R. V. Cassill, copyright © 1969 by Bantam Books, Inc. "Poem" (While the dead jay) first appeared in Nickel Review.

ROBERT MEZEY. "In This Life" first appeared in Kayak. "Last Words" was published as a booklet of the same title by The Cummington Press, 1970. "Kaleidoscope" first appeared in Kayak.

KHATCHIK MINASIAN. The poems from *The Simple Songs of Khatchik Minasian* are reprinted by permission of the author. "Beyond the Gage" first appeared in Lines.

DeWAYNE RAIL. "House" first appeared in Tennesse Poetry Journal.

DENNIS SALEH. "A Guide to Familiar American Incest" first appeared in The North American Review, copyright 1968 by the University of Northern Iowa. "The Thumb" first appeared in Kayak. "Frankenstein's Journal" first appeared in the Beloit Poetry Journal.

HERBERT SCOTT. "Late Fall, Setting Traps" first appeared in Poetry, 1969, copyright 1969 by The Modern Poetry Association. Reprinted with permission of the author and of the editor of Poetry. "Passing the Masonic Home for the Aged" first appeared in The North American Review, copyright 1969 by the University of Northern Iowa. "The Man in the Closet" first appeared in Poetry Northwest. "Spring Commences" first appeared in the Massachusetts Review. "Excavations" first appeared in The Southern Review. "The Apprentice Grave Digger" first appeared in the Massachusetts Review. "Picture Puzzle" first appeared in the Beloit Poetry Journal.

FOREWARD

The poets of this anthology have at one time or another passed through, stayed or left a place called Fresno. They have all remained long enough to be touched by the landscape, hear the noises of the people, and then write. The voices of the poems are the poets'; their voices are the story of this book.

David Kherdian
James Baloian

Fresno, California
February 6, 1970

Poets missing from the cover photo: William Childress, Robert L. Jones, Larry Levis and Herbert Scott.

Poets added: William Everson and William Saroyan.

CONTENTS

LAWSON INADA

GARY JOHNSON

ROBERT L. JONES

DAVID KHERDIAN

HERBERT SCOTT

ROBERTA SPEAR

Down at the Santa Fe Depot:
20 Fresno Poets

JAMES BALOIAN

Tom Peck

I was born August 11, 1945 in Fresno, and have been stuck here now for 24 years, with occasional escapes to different States, and Canada & Mexico.

Got lucky, married, and left for two years to live in southern California.

One baby girl and a snow dog.

Since then have done many things to keep as far away from Fresno as I can, but so far stuck, but deeply in love with the earth, and the great family which is this book.

UP TO MEZEY'S

up past
the first fields
of dead grass
            the slow
    rise of hills
    opening green,
    shifting winds,
            crossing animals
    risking blank turns

        the closed houses
            blinking whites and blues

            up past the flatness
                the late summer
            we meet—
            his short arms
            opened
                    into flight

he whispers
  and in that moment
  grabs my hand and leads
  me back
back from the first front of trees
        back
        into everything growing

LOVE POEM

we slept in the grass
too tired to move
or clean the ground
of branches
and dirt still wet
with the dark

underneath roots push
like streams

to the sea
i want to stick
my whole head
in and follow

THE INDIANS

Taking all the phones
in his hands, he told
them he wouldn't be
available for questioning.
He knew he could
shut the windows,
and no one would come to his door.
He even
bought a gun,
insisting that the only
noises he could hear
were the naked feet
of indians, coal black and hunched,
circling the edge
of his burning field.

THE CHURCH

it's all too careful
even the mouse
living beneath
the statue of christ
is mad

he is a fist of nerves
running
silently

HAWK

in the distance
rain falling
only limp hands
drag the air

palms open
and black from picking

WHAT MOVES

For My Wife

at dark they come pushing up
from kitchens
the butchers, the old women with broken knives
and with each twist they create the real

        of what you believe
        of believe

        of what moves

LOVE POEM

the leaves
their golden bodies
shattered below the trees

the boy left
to keep watch
is sleeping in a field
children watching him
      dance around him

the moon is fat yellow

the boy dreams of snow
and so far into a field
when he turns for light

the field is darkness

THE DEATH OF AN ALASKAN ESKIMO

When the snow runs wild in November
the sea seems to freeze and stop,
and new winds break over his house.
He is Igwa, Alaskan Eskimo;
born animal in the cave below the ground.
He talked to the seal on the ocean,
watched the caribou mate and fawn.

When he saw the first steps
of the wooden building and watched
the hooded robes stare at him in despair,
he arose from the cave;
his lungs breathe new air
and collapsed the next winter.

When they buried him under the ice,
the ground inherited him, the snow blew wild.
Igwa was blessed three times
for being a lamb, while the caribou
mated and the seal talked.

THE TRAIN

naked she stumbles
through the dark
making familiar excuses
she admits nothing
not even the darkness
or my wet fingers
the constant rain

of her black forest
makes everything grow
my teeth snap
my tongue whistles
like a train
old men raise
their heads from
fifty-years sleep
to watch
the engine push deeper

THE BEATING

up from palm street
and down to where

the trees darken
everything

and the moon
a ripe orange

sits in the mouth
of a young boy

being beaten to death
what the murderers

take from him is
his pig look

swollen cheeks
and an orange

stuck with diamonds

WHAT THE BLIND DREAM OF

there is a difference
of flesh

of how far
to step

of whose words
you should

listen to next
and always

the edge
of your own hands —

two stumps
growing eyes

blind as your own

LOVE POEM

For Levine

   i said
here are the hands
you wanted
the rest are coming

there is even
a boy who plays
the violin in a field
no one has been
able to stop him

no one ever will

WAKING

the alley
grows thin
in the face of the moon
my eyes close
so i can look
backward

the road
pressed between clouds
opens its palm
of flashing rabbits
and deer
my body comes
hurling like a star
through this town
fists and lungs

screaming
for air

B. H. BOSTON

Tom Peck

I was born in Oakland, California on June 24, 1946 and have lived in California ever since. Twelve years in Walnut Creek where I remember Elvis Presley and Cheri Esquibel, three years in Colusa where most of puberty was spent in a kayak on the Sacramento River longing for a different ancestry, one year in Sanger where I met Marsha, and seven years in Fresno where we began a family, graduated from college, and learned that occasionally poetry means what it says. We now reside in Laguna Beach, California (not far from the University of California at Irvine) struggling to live at least one decibel above the obscene roar of weekend tourism and general Orange County earth/mind fuck. I have left California only twice: once for Las Vegas to be married and once for Oregon with my grandparents to visit the Oregon Caves. I have always wanted to travel.

MONTANA'S APRIL THAW

Dusk-grey and swollen,
the river enters into snowbanks,
widening to the iced trunk
of a fallen oak,
to dark openings in the landscape
where drifts have melted,
where the glazed tissues of last year's leaves
thicken, exposed.

A light rain begins to fall,
congesting the air with silence.
I think of November,
of a mallard,
starved, disoriented,
swallowing a branch,
of the last flight,
and the quiet.

As the water moves into blackness
and the damp wind shudders
in the tops of the nearest trees,
I turn back to the house,
frozen to this promise
of an early Spring,
to this feeding of one
season on another.

ANOTHER DAY

> *Keeping score in times of war*
> *takes a superman.*
>> —Country Joe and the Fish

Cruising over the hills,
I realize how late I am.
I slept deep in the earth
and stayed longer than I knew.
My suit is still clean.

To the south, the fog
has lifted from the marshes.
Sunlight spreads over the fields
and dusted trees. From here,
last night's abandoned dead
lie like thumbs in the black mud.

To the north, I think,
I hear a woman whispering prayers
in her native language,
a language I have learned.
She would love to kneel
at the huge white face
of a dead president.

There are other voices.
The morning moves around me,
flushing my clever senses.
This has never happened before.
I have lost count.
I must turn and drill into the sun.

SEPTEMBER 22

The old man next door
who has no voice but a note pad
and cannot hear, who lives

in a range of wind and difficult cars,
could not know that today
the stadium in town
is full of children.

He knows little of children.
He was caught early and counselled
and has none.

To fake a living, he paints
signs and sells them to his sister—
No Dancing or Loitering Here,
Bar Closed, Stay Away—This evening
as the blunt shadows spread
toward my open porch, he stops
to remind me of Christ's Crusade
coming up on T.V. He marks
his place, and we smile,

and I think that someday
this heavy old man will fall
on his bed of dormant bulbs
and lie between our houses
like a larva or cocoon,
like something in its final stages
turning to nothing without wings.

AFTER ALL

The rain filters
like blood
through the loose basins of my hands.
Thunderheads numb the ridges,
the air clears.
The shadows flex
and sink into the valley,
into memories of fields and tall grass.

I step quietly
from mountain to mountain,
hunting the smooth hills

for bits of silk, links of bone braced
against no wind,
for the last flight out of the floodlands
left astounded in the scorched trees.

I gather what I can,
what I remember.
I have written her name
across the swamp of the Midwest.
I have built mounds of stone
near the hot gauze of the sky.
I pluck the scar on my wrist.

We are finally naked.
It is the second Spring.
Nothing has changed.

THE SAVAGE, OUR FATHERS

for Levine

plateaus
the trunks of enormous
trees in the sun
the dark obsidian body
the shrug behind stones
the insistent clatter of the fields

in breechcloth
in feathers brilliant
with Jesuit blood
the plotting of
horizons
their commitment to memory

* * *

there is no place
to go and not be
in hiding

14 B. H. BOSTON

the mountains are ragged
the mountains do not follow one another
beneath the pale sky
helicopters dare the canyons
into war

for a moment
the blades flicker across
her forehead
my feet
covered and trembling in the dust

I AM READING

in the kitchen
to my wife—
the newspaper, a poem,
anything to calm her.

Between each page
she walks to the window
and scans the yard
for our daughter—
outside, playing.

No, the other children
are good to her:
they pull her by turns
in the wagon;
they have stopped
taking her toys . . .

But earlier, she
came running into
the house, laughing,
bleeding where a dog
had bitten her, just
above the ear—
a dog as big as I.

WILLIAM CHILDRESS

Robert Oakes

Born in Hugo, Oklahoma, in 1933 to migrant worker parents, I spent my youth in cottonfields in Oklahoma, Texas, Arizona, and California. In 1951, I escaped into the Army, which was so much better I stayed 7 years. Korea nailed me in 1952; I went as a Demolitions Expert, and learned to love plastic explosives, which we burned to keep warm. I secret couriered for awhile, then was discharged after the war in 1953. Entered a barber school, which proved to be a hair shirt—I starved for awhile, then re-upped in the paratroops, where I made 33 jumps—all terrifying. But fun, too. The next 3 years, in Germany and later outside Paris, I packed giant parachutes for a Heavy-Drop unit. Objective in war: To bring down tanks and guns in one piece so they can fulfill their mission of making people into pieces. I'm rabidly antiwar, and marched in the huge Washington Peace March—the one where Nixon watched football, while city buses made an iron ring, bumper to bumper, around the White House. Discharged in 1958, I re-enlisted in the USAF, but disgustedly got out of that the next year. Tried to write, couldn't, enrolled in Fresno State College where I was able to study poetry and fiction writing. Paul Engle got me a grant to The Writer's Workshop, U. of Iowa, in 1966 and two years later I had an M.F.A. Have published poems, stories, articles and essays in magazines, and a TV-thing for *Daktari*. Currently, I'm an Editor-Writer for *National Geographic* in Washington. I'm married and have one son.

NOTE FROM A PART-TIME NEGRO

1970: Paranoid,
I tear another year from my life
and stare at the fog that hides the dirt
beyond my window. A room away, my wife
sleeps and dreams of spiders, pregnant
with another number for IBM.
The child will be born a natural card,
under Aries, the sign of the Ram.
I would weep for it if I could weep,
but tears are as sporadic as sleep
anymore, and as a rule induced
only by country clubs and tear gas,
or my numbered days on calenders.
Yes, I'm sick, but no more than those
who write in toilets, "Nixon eats Niggers."
A little grass, some acid, I make my way,
and every year become a little larger.

SOLDIER'S LEAVE

Beside the river where he walks,
boulders like green and moldy loaves
resist the downward pull of water
and hold their own in ordered grooves.

It is October, and the leaves,
once so flexible and green,
grate on each other in the wind
like a surgeon's knife on bone.

Soon ice will form among the trees
in lean and ash-grey splinters,
but he will be gone before it does
on a cold campaign of winter's.

THE WARLOCK

In his Edgar Poe house,
in a secret place,
he keeps the shapes
he conjures. The room holds
demons he can't hold,
and turns none loose.

Yet last night he dreamed
soft shuddering wings
and woke to find them real.
A furry demon
attacked his lamp and him.
He killed it with a broom.

Omens are only omens
and dreams just dreams,
but now he wonders
at the room above the stairs,
and studies his ancient book
afraid to look.

Magicians, too, wait
days tomorrow
may be, bringing a sun to melt
curses deeper than marrow.
He brews what he has to brew.
The days pass like hearses.

THE PUSHER

DuPont Circle squares off at night,
giving it to the straight world straight.
Shuffling figures with arms like reeds,
pus-filled veins, and eyes of paste
are making for you and making haste,
hawking their lust for wine or speed.

Gaunt black ghosts whose dismal
sermons speak of coming fear
surround the fountain. Baptismal
rites are solemnized among gowns
dark as their wearers, gentlemen
whose eyes freeze out laughter.

And then there is me, running
after whatever keeps running away.
Only I'm you, and the habit you say
you've kicked and haven't. In my eyes,
the silver stalks of needles shine,
promising light for the coming day.

VAMPIRE

Always it was my shadow.
It had ways of leaving
without asking leave,
and always, grieving
was sure to follow. Someone
would grieve a woman

I'd never heard of, and reveal
her sad fate to others.
And each night, something killed;
something frightful and dark stalked
the city, and no one dared
to ask about its diet.

I did all I could. Nothing.
The things my shadow did weren't mine.
Yet I've been finding stains
on shirts I know I've worn,
and why memories of screams
slowly pooling in my mind?

They cornered it at last,
tracked it to this old house
and to a kind of dusty chest.
I was as proud as anyone
to see them poise a wooden fang
and drive it home, bit by bit,

and though I felt no sympathy,
the devil knows I felt pain.
But all that was months ago.
Now I sit inside, listening to rain
lamenting, and to the dry rustle
of my shadow, growing like a tail.

THE ADDICT

From the steel window, stained with the dust
of autumn winds, he watches the night
peel from the sky like dead skin. The season
turns pastures to rust and brings no heat,
and under his feet, the stone floor is cold.

Some have said a longing of the mind
keeps him alive, and ease his pain
by settling with a delicate rain

the thin dust of his dreams. At the edge
of his illusionary world

soft walls keep him from harm. God insists
that this be so, and in his green gown,
pads through secret porticoes and halls,
and brings a shining needle, and is kind.

FOR MY SON

Shadows of trenchcoats darken
his crib; tiny fingers grope
towards a future of steel
cables on a ship's deck,
weighted duffel, and arms
that drag him downward.

I see his small skull bound
in iron confinement; the
doll's face pressed
to his mother's breast
darkens like crisped leather

in a flamethrower's blast.
Trenchfoot and worms,
wounds spilling gangrene,
delicate skin torn
by shrapnel. And then,

his eyes empty as spent
cartridges, he is packaged
for home. These are the
gifts of male birthdays,
wrapped in patriot slogans,
and sent by lying leaders.

Happy birthday to you,
Happy birthday to you,
Happy birthday my son,
Happy birthday to you.

MICHAEL CLIFTON

Tom Peck

I was born in Reedley, Calif., on January 6, 1949. My parents were both born in Oklahoma and made the trip from the Dust Bowl in the 1930's. My father lied about his age to join the Army and ended up as a career officer, so our family moved around with him on his different tours of duty.

I went through junior high and high school in Fresno and occupied myself with reading and trying to ignore school. I started writing poetry about halfway through my senior year in high school, because I was bored and poetry helped. Then I sort of fell into the writing program at Fresno State College, and, with the invaluable help and guidance of a couple of different people, I've been writing ever since.

BARRACKS

I remember the barracks
with wooden steps
naked as ladders
racking the walls
pretending nothing.

I grew up
in buidings like that
knocking up and
down the stairs.

Two-and-a-half
trying to balance
on the edge of a porch
and my own fear
I fell two stories
and lived:
a support broke my fall
to the concrete.

My life given back to me
by the barracks.

In Germany
I was older.

There were carpets
and china now
even crystal.

Workmen started pouring
blacktop for clotheslines
and left a pile
behind the building.

One of us ran to the top
stuck there crying
and wrenched his foot
from his shoe
to get out.

He never got out.

Like the rest of us
struck stiff
between the barracks.

THREADS

A man moves toward me
as the light pours itself
into deep pools.

His face, almost familiar, flickers
like water waving around rocks.

He sits near me
with his back turned,
his head between his knees;
I can count the knobs on his spine
pushing out the skin like knuckles.

Our silence is that quiet
woven into leaves and long grass.

The air darkens and I feel myself
stretched lean as the wind slicing
between two feathers of a wing.

FOR KENNY WATKINS

   (Middleweight boxing champion of California, 1942)

We meet across the counter in the airport,
the terminal an arena almost empty
of lights and the voices
always just beyond, the ones with money,
the ones he couldn't see to fight.

He must have been heavier before.
The meat hangs slack on his frame,

strung between bones swollen
with years of voices
outside the lights.

He stands there in a thin wool coat
hunting them now, says
he collects bills and then,
"It's like fighting—
if you wear them down you can beat them
every time."

And then he's gone,
treading the linoleum toward another voice,
this one in L.A. and all the others
to wear out until his bones,
grown huge under the skin,
burst back into light.

POEM FOR "PAPA BEAR"

Some men won't skin a bear
after they've killed it:
without the hide it looks
too much like a man.

I've seen my father look like that:
pale, terribly human as he pauses
and swings his head into the wind,
hunting for the smell of ice
from some mountain where cave-mouths glitter
and gape like open graves.

He runs naked from the sharp years;
clever hunters have flayed the fur
from his shoulders and soft belly
in strips so thin it's taken this long
to finish it.

GLOVER DAVIS

Tom Peck

I was born in 1939 in San Luis Obispo. The things that I remember most were the troop trains with columns of frightened men lining the windows, and tanks coming down the streets of that town at night. And then the long, bad dream of childhood, endless boarding schools, fist fights that I hated, the wasted time in the usual bad american high school where the only thing I liked was football and 3 years in the navy worse than high school, Fresno State and poetry, scattering a group of high school teacher night students on my motor cycle with Dennis Saleh and outrunning the campus police. I teach poetry at San Diego State and try to live as much as possible like a digger Indian on land halfway to the desert.

THE GIANT

"It's difficult being a giant."

Robert Mezey

When I step, my heel
sputters with what's
pinned under it

and I can't help
imagining the thousands
of mouths paying

out blood, and the stunned
faces. But I need
water, air, light

and it takes meat
to make the muscles
ripple along my arm

to make the flesh
come back after
centuries of sleep.

When I jounce myself
tatoos quiver
like painted ribbons.

I touch the flag
of blood that coils
my throat

the medals of honor
that roll and bounce
in an ocean

of lard.
I make sure
that I'm all here

and greasy coins
that pouch between my legs
spurt oil, rubber, steel.

THE PILOT

Takes my hand
and the syllables slip
from his burned mouth

like compressed air.
Dazed by whiskey
he speaks of water

of the gray
fields of the sea
which mean safety

and of the villages
he never sees, rocked
in a dream of fire.

His hands balance
like wings showing
me that angle

where bodies lighten
and eyes stream with fire.
When I close my eyes

I see dust spurt
from his goggles
or dance like flame

along the clear
panels of plexiglass.
"Touch me, he says,

touch me when I sleep
or when I dream."
When I touched him

he was five. I am his mother
and I paint the bad knee
that bled and bled.

ANONYMOUS PHONECALLS

The girl across the table rattles
       a porcelain cup.
Her fear moves across her eyes like wind
       over water
or her hand across a pane of clear glass.

She takes off her tinted contact
       lenses and her eyes
change color-green beneath silver.
       The black centers
push pencilled islands outward toward
       the whitening edges.

2.

       Sometimes, late at night
she phones me anonymously, and
       I feel her voice slide
like a glass wave and gain momentum.
       Something calls me so
quietly that it's just below anything
       I can hear. It's soft
as flame wearing through cellophane and
       the things that aren't said
pass through the air in needles of silence.
       Her breathing's regular
and smooth. It seems to indicate pain,
       and it comes coursing
over the wires, rippling a long rope
       one end in her hand
and one end in mine. Her voice
       is rich and deep and
it swells like a column of blood,
       spinning blackened coins
across the disks of microphones,
       circulating strands
of smoke through the hot circles of her throat.

3.

I speak from a pocket of darkness
          near the telephone;
echoes come back like sonar,
          and I can tell that
she's finished. I can tell that she's let
          the blunt receiver
slip from her hand, down the bedspread where
          it corkscrews on
the end of the cord, where the great lips char
          in the searing wind
that rushes from the mouthpiece.

FROM THE DARK ROOM

People buy sun glasses, beer, oil their skins
and change their clothes like elms putting up shields
of green, but still the heat presses. I wince
as every sonic boom shakes trays, and winds

seem to sweep out of the dark; the red that glows
from the ceiling light dances across the waves
until my rubbered hand stops everything.
I see the world in pictures. When light flows

through delicate patterns of leaves or clouds
they stiffen and wait for the thunder. But the film
is there like raw tissue open to the light.
I see in photos, people strung in crowds

on the beaches, in the streets, on the pavements
black with heat where people run and are caught
by bursts of flashbulbs, or where alone and guilty
they turn on their lives in these explosive moments.

They seem the same, unlike the bulbs that heat
has left clouded and split with veins. But I
am here alone as always, feeling fine.
I turn from my work a few times a day to eat.

I noticed yesterday the negative
of school children caught at play, their features
like charcoal, their hair, lips, and eyes a luminous
expanding white, the sky black and tentative.

BANDAGING BREAD

for Leon

"Police will cluster
along the borders of the ghettos.
The precincts will pulse like wounded flies.
People, are burning," L says,
"everything rocks in a film of heat."
He lifts two loaves of black bread
from the map on his kitchen table.
"This bread is taped like dynamite
for the C.I.A. is everywhere
and we must practice.
The time is coming,
we cannot hold it back,
when the wounds of the table
will swell like blossoms.
The time is coming," he says
pointing to a bridge
"a loaf here
and the bridge will rise like dust,
the suburbs will settle and fill with light."

PETER EVERWINE

Tom Peck

Born in Detroit, Michigan, 1930. Afterwards, he thought this was the reason for recurring fits of depression.

He dreamed of being victimized by hostile automobiles. Raised in western Pennsylvania, he went to various schools and drifted through the army. From his education he discovered the value of disguise.

He became a monologist.

He thought of himself as the duke of dark corners.

Back in schools after the army, he wrote his first poems.

He dreamed of striking back.

Then he discovered the perfect marriage of form and content: He was silent.

Thus he became an agent of the dead letter office and discovered the value of rumor. The next step was inevitable: he entered teaching—first at Iowa, then at Fresno.

He became unAmerican.

In 1968, in a Mexican cantina, he suffered a conversion under a portrait of Pancho Villa and went back to writing poems in order to understand silence.

It is taking a long time.

He has been blessed with good friends; two sons, Christopher and David; and the two women who bore them, Katharine and Sandra.

HOME FROM DUCK MARSH

All day in the rain and sour reek
Of the marsh, in the fluttering grasses of killdeer,
All day I have been speaking
In the tongues of duck, squalling in joy
Of smartweed, watershield, salt hay,
As the green brows of mallards rode
In the high winds.

It is evening now, it is weariness;
It is the weight of the body deepening
Into the pools of rain,
Into the clear dark eyes of birds.
Around me the cities are stoking-up for
The night, the furnaces singing of death
Until the old are stunned with it,
And the young before their banked altars of sound
Hum like wires in the wastes of Kansas.

But it is evening now, it is weariness.
The bittern descends for the last time
And the egret closes its whiteness in the tall grass.
And in this quiet house of rain
I am the last sane man on earth,
Sleep settling on my brow
Like a great crown.

THE MARSH, NEW YEAR'S DAY

For Zack, among others

The slow, cold breathing.
Black surf of birds lifting away.
The light rising in the water's skin.
How many times now, on a day like this,
I've entered the celebrations of the reeds,
Waking by the wren's broken house,
The frosty, burst phallus of the cat-tail.
In the marsh, a door slams and slams.
I want to open my throat
And sing the crystal song of the goose.
Wherever I look,
I see the old men
Of my boyhood, wifeless and half-wild,
In stained coats, dying like rainbows
From the feet up.
I am becoming them.

WE MEET IN THE LIVES OF ANIMALS

In Mexico, a red flag in the market signifies
freshly butchered meat. *Maggie's drawers* is
the red flag flown on army firing ranges.

1.

The red flag is up.
The beasts who came down to market
From the high fields of light
Sprawl heavy from hooks, yellow
With fat, spread-legged,
Still beaded with blood.
Having been gentle,
They came easily.
Having opened their breasts,

34 PETER EVERWINE

They give up everything—heart, kidneys,
Flecked lungs, the frothy dark rivers of organs,
Self-stink of panic and shit—
Shameless, without malice.
Even the flies enter them like hives.

2.

In the dirt yard next door
The widow Tomasa has fired-up
Her steaming pot. She calls out,
And my son goes running.
"Here," she says, cradling
A cow's bloody head from which she scrapes
It's stringy flesh. "Here,
Hold open its eyes.
It will see our hunger."
And my son's eyes fill, as he touches
Those milky ones.

They're poor, I tell him later.

3.

He weeps and has bad dreams.
It will pass. He will eat meat
As his father does, will come to hunger
And boast like other men: I'll tear the asshole
Out of skunk! Murder the beaver's balls!
Chew knuckles! Gnaw on the goose's glands,
The peacock's gristle!
The red flag is up, is waving.
Maggie's drawers fill with blood.
The angel in the *Wehrmacht* helmet
Goes down on her, eating the ripe lips.
Banging our empty bowls
We come before the lives of animals,
Greeting them with nails and empty palms
As they come marching, marching
In their bloody rags.

And still he weeps.

4.

At the jaw's hinge
My son has a soft blond down I love to touch.
It is the delicate grass
In which a lion sleeps, the silken weeds
Where the crow comes to walk.
A man comes from his own murders
And enters a pasture
In which the grass is filling with light.
He hears a quiet footfall and turns.
And it is something like love.

COLLECTING THE ANIMALS AT ACADEMY, CALIFORNIA

First the horses left the pasture,
Rattling away in the old truck.
No one will wake now
In the night, hearing their hard
Hammers beat the ground, the wind
Shake-out their violence
To the hunched stony hills.

Then the peacocks
Closed their eyes in the dust.
Day after day they moved
In the dead grass like portions
Of the sea, like blue stones praising
The coals of heaven.

At last even the guinea hens
Who blazed and gabbled in the oak at sundown
Dropped like gray fruit
And were gathered in.
So it was done.

Let the pasture lie empty,
The light fall undisturbed
On the bare fields.
What were the animals but ourselves
Flashing with the wind, stripped-down,
Simple at last—the lives

That go on evading us, yet move
In shadows at the field's edge, in trees
Flowing away like water on the far hills.
And what is there to grieve?
Here are the tracks they made
In this place.

THE HEAVY ANGEL

Muffled against the chill of the salt slough
You step from a mist so shot with light,
So empty of horizon, that it seems
You are adrift—a heavy angel
Falling in a place hardly a place
But only this luminous swirl touched
By a few brown stalks.
On the water your bright shape
Ripples about your ankles as if, in falling,
You entered your own wavering brilliance,
The body deepening to its most lucid image.
Why is it you come so quietly,
Always when I least expect you?

Sometimes at night
When the city breathes against the window
And my hand closes like a stone
I seek you down the acrid street of the dead fathers
Or in the dark lakes of the child I was,
Sensing your presence then, the shadow
You make behind my closed lid.
But it is here I know you best,
Surprise you in the solitary places,
My boots sinking in the dark muck
And the snipe leaping from the grass
Crying its shrill *scape, scape.*
And I bend to meet you,
My likeness, my heavy angel,
Seeing as if for the first time
Your face wild and shining,
Still wet with the sea.

LOOKING INTO THINGS CLEARLY

The doctor smiles and comes toward me.
In a room so pure I can hardly breathe,
He opens my robe and touches the fragile
Bones of my wings. "I'm glad you've come," he says,
And I know I'm sick.

Something is wrong with me upstairs.
A neighbor's mouth tears like a wound, so dark
I think of a spring cupped in black roots.
The phone rings and another village is burning.
My head dreams of escaping into a white stone.

"It's almost painless," he says, hiding
His hand behind his blue coat.
Only I can't see him clearly.
When I squint, he seems to be
My father sidling through the halls of banks,

He is a bruised face, he is the President,
The drifting blue haze of factories,
Of my breath hovering over me.
I reach to touch him, but my fingers
Enter and pass through—

He blossoms around them in a red flower of light,
Petal after petal of light opens out:
I'm at a window looking into a backyard.
Some men are digging what looks like a grave,
About the size of a child's.

LIVING BY WATER

All morning the lake trembles,
Opening and closing its palms.
An old woman enters its shallows, stiffly
Like a hunched black heron,
Her dress floating out
Until she moves in her own heavy cloud,

One among many.
The lake opens and closes its palms.
It is late evening.
Already the reeds are pulsing
With the blood of stars.

PERHAPS IT'S AS YOU SAY

Perhaps it's as you say
That nothing stays lost forever

How many times have I said No No
There is a darkness in the cell

And opened my hands to cup emptiness
Tasting its bitten face

I do not know if our loves survive us
Waiting through the long night for our step

Or if they will know us then
Entering our flesh with the old sigh

I do not know
But I think of fields that stretch away flat

Beneath the stars their dry grasses
Gathering a light of honey

The few houses wink and go out
Across the fields an asphalt road darkens

And disappears among the cottonwoods by the dry creek
It is so quiet so quiet

Meet me there

C. G. HANZLICEK

I was born on August 23, 1942, in Owatonna, Minnesota. The town was named after an Indian princess, but of course I never saw an Indian in the seventeen years I lived there. I later came across a few Indians harvesting wild rice on the lakes near the Canadian border and a far greater number of them on Minneapolis' skid row, the last reservation granted them by a city that could find no use for them. The missions along East Hennepin Avenue were the storehouses of Minnesota's greatest cultural dowery. So it goes.

I attended the University of Minnesota from 1960-64. While there I took every course I could get from the poet James Wright, a man who could turn a classroom into a magic circle. I had never seen anything like it, and I haven't since. Whatever intensities of emotion I have experienced in recent years can almost certainly be traced back to that time when James Wright shook me awake from a deep Midwestern sleep. No small shake: that hibernal catatonia so common in Minnesota is the only protection against sub-zero weather and sub-zero quality of life.

From Minneapolis I went to to Iowa City, Iowa, and studied in the Writers Workshop for two years. The weather improved slightly, but Iowa City is a strange place. Many of its inhabitants commit suicide. Or murder. Or rape. Or simply sock themselves in the eye. Any sort of violence will do. Marvin Bell was my teacher, friend and pinball opponent in Iowa City. From Marvin I learned that the first draft of a poem is usually nothing more than a socially acceptable form of masturbation. He taught me the patience to revise.

I came to teach at Fresno State College in 1966. Fresno has been good to me. It's such a dull, dull town that I've had time to write. Fresno has also been good to me in that it gave me a big, beautiful, blonde wife who has stopped my head's habit of bouncing against the wall.

My first collection of poems, LIVING IN IT, will be published in the summer of 1970 by The Stone Wall Press.

THE DAY WE'VE ALL BEEN WAITING FOR

The radar of the bats
Has failed at last.
They have lost their hunger,

And the insects hum as peacefully
As little girls
Pretending to be good.

Surely this is our season
And our sign.

Now we can afford to count.
We drop beads into a black box,
One bead for each of our sins.

The iron clappers of the bells
Are insistent
As a head against a madhouse wall:

We have been forgiven.

In concrete pockets
Of power dams
The bones of workmen who fell

Stand at attention
For the call to rise.

THE SMUGGLER

> *for Bruce*

Mexican hotels have the best
Walls
The liveliest shows

That crack is a river
It is a border
Two bad countries

And roach man will get shot
By a frightened cop
In the belly crossing

Look at that arm
Gray and hard as wood

Knock I will not open
Not to you cop
Not tonight

Look at that arm
What can you do with it

Fallen veins
Saying no more no more

And you said I couldn't
Afford it
A body is cheap the cheapest

If I had some water
My tongue
Would weigh less than a pound

So I should get up
I should get going
Swing these arms like lumber

Churn toward that borderline
Moving

O man will I be moving
My asshole full
Of heroin

THE ALLIGATOR BOY

We have paid a quarter to see
His skin.
We can touch it if we like.

It is tough and dark
As an old boot and doesn't feel

The hatpins,
The knifeblades,
The heated darning needles,

And if his fingers tremble,
The barker says, it is

Not from pain
But shyness.

We can touch him if we like.

TO MY WIFE

Whenever you are like this—

The flesh around your eyes blotched
By red islands from silent
Weeping in the bathroom,

And your words and that vision you had
Stuck in your chest like a sparrow
In a car's grille—

I do the easiest thing:

I toss my body out of the cockpit
And fly my wreckage into the sun.

LIVING IN IT

The radio is on.
The radio is on and on and on . . .

I have, perhaps, learned
How to live in it.

Learned hunger from the open
Mouths
Of red filaments.

Learned energy from the low
Voltage hum behind my body.

The news announcer says
There has been a prison
Break in Atlanta.

I do not believe him.

The weatherman says it will
Rain tonight and then freeze solid,
And no doors will break

The walls of ice.
Yes, that is more likely.

My father will be caught
In the tool factory,
Limping across oily floors

In steel-toed safety shoes.
His hands were never safe:

He has a finger
Missing from his right hand
And knuckles

Like oak knots.
Father,

He is my father,
Locked in the factory,

Locked in my flat voice,
Chain smoking Pall Malls and picking

His way across the slick floors
Of poems
That do no justice.

LAWSON INADA

Tom Peck

I'm a Sansei, and was born in Fresno in 1938. Father's people were sharecroppers but he became a dentist. Mother's father started the Fresno Fish Store. During the War we lived in "camps" in Fresno, Arkansas, and Colorado.

After the War, I went to Lincoln, then Edison High School. A non-Buddhist, I joined the Black and Chicano set. The main thing then was music: Johnny Ace, The Clovers, Little Walter, etc., and on into Pres and Bird. They made me want to "say" something.

After a year at Fresno State, I went to Cal (The Black Hawk, actually) and saw The Lady, Bud, Miles, and Coltrane, so when I got back to State I was studying the bass. Then Phil Levine got me interested in writing.

The bass became lost during subsequent stays in New York, New England, and the Midwest, but there are three Inadas with me now: Janet and the boys—Miles and Lowell.

We're living in Oregon, listening to the Great Ones and singing. I've completed one book, The Great Bassist. "West Side Songs" are from a work-in-progress, The Death of Coltrane.

WEST SIDE SONGS

I. WHITERARAMA

Catch the skyline, baby—
Security, Towne House,
P. G. & E.

Know what I mean?
That's Whitearama, baby,
the big wide screen.

II. SOMETHING HOLDS

Something holds
it in place.
Something keeps it
from exploding.
Otherwise, it would be
all wars rolled
into one—Mexicans
punctured on chopsticks,

Blacks gagging
on crucifixes, curses
croaking in broken
English . . .

But wait . . .

That's why the railroad
snakes through
the town like a fence.

That's why they
toss in a few
wigs and grey suits

and sit, and wait.

III. PURPLE

Purple
the grape.
Purple
the mind
aged
in wine.
Purple
the vine
wine
cannot
puncture.
Purple
the face
burning
on trays
of new
empty
lots of
purple
Urban Renewal.

IV. "SUNSET"

The sun never sets
on the Mexican
section—"Sunset."
Big street lights
keep them awake,
out of trouble,
fingering the hoes
of Mexican golf.
Mexicans commute
to find trouble.
They sing. They cut.
At wrestling arenas,
Mexicans beat
the bad Japanese.
Mexicans are fun.

The sun never sets
on the Mexican
section. It never comes up.

V. "JERICHO"

"Jericho's"
a citadel,
slab of plaster
by the Black villas
by the slaughterhouse
by the city dump.

Policedogs keep
vigil—
sniffing out
White men, a minstrel cop.

Upstairs, slabs
on the racks.
You can stab them
and giggle.

You can get in
and wiggle.

Downstairs, the dice's
mammy grin.
The juke box
squeals the blues—
drunk
on a funky
harmonica.

Blackies stay happy.

Mornings, when Black
garbagemen come,
they play
buckets
like drums.

Sometimes, a Black
foetus dances
out in the gutter,
with ribs.

Come on over
and wail—

"Jericho", slaughterhouse,
dump.

VI. OKIES

I always thought an Okie
was a white man gone fake—
play-acting, a spy.

Now I know Okies
are okay.
They dig music.
They cut each other up.

VII. ARMENIANS

are screwed up.
I mean
they won't move
to the West Side.
They're known
as the Fresno Jews.

They're screwed up.
I mean
they shave
names and noses
and herd hairy
Mustangs to school.

VIII. HE-RO

You know
about the sound
barrier.
Well don't you know
Willie broke
the color
barrier screaming
through White town
with a White girl
at 95 per.

After
the funeral,
his Cadillac
hub-caps flew
over in formation,
in tribute.

IX. FILIPINOS

are sharp.
That's why
they're barbers.
Sharp
trousers,
sharp
elevator shoes.
When they see
White girls
they go
"Sook sook sook sook."

X. CHINKS

Ching Chong Chinaman
sitting on a fence
trying to make a dollar
chop-chop all day.

"Eju-kei-shung! Eju-kei-shung!"
that's what they say.

When the War came,
they said, "We Chinese!"
When we went away,
they made sukiyaki,
saying, "Yellow all same."

When the war closed,
they stoned the Japs' homes.

Grandma would say:
"Marry a Mexican,
a Nigger, just don't
marry no Chinese."

Last of the Mohicans & grew secretly wild. In high school I got a car, went to work in my father's grocery store & read behind the meat-case. In college I lived in a moldy bomb shelter, gave up meat, & wrote about a woman who is good for me.

Now I'm living with her and my little boy Mana in the Sierra foot-hills.

When I'm in my natural head poems are the eyes of stones & animals. They teach me to keep my eyes open.

FROM ADAM'S SIDE AND EVE'S SONG

On the mountain cold drizzle falling with dawn
I ate wild honey over the fire
It is too late to clear the ground
I lost my way, rain in my head
carving the refugees of your world in a book
I stood on the clouds
searching for eyes without fear

I talked to the river:
        I am alive and dead flowing thru space
        living and dying day after day
a voice said come with me for a new name
let the book fall to the sky

spinning round and round on the wings
        of a swastika
we swam toward the ripples in my young face
I came from the water opened to receive my mother
in flames from the other side of the earth
just appearing over ancient mountains
erupted from fissures in my body

SONG

O new day breaking
stars made invisible
the earth falling like a crumb
from the great mouth

PRAYING MANTIS

After hearing the truth
it's hard to come back
and live as if we had time for it

onions and cabbage need weeding
there's firewood to cut
Anna washes clothes
feeds Mana at her nipples
and I go on gathering
crumbs thrown down for the hungry

living up here, away from people in cities
days go by
and I don't think about them . . .

but sometimes at dusk
when silence covers these hills
I feel like a thief

so I climb the mountain
to watch the sun fold like an eagle's wing

and drift in his loose feathers until
I hear a tiny voice . . .
and squat with shaky knees

remember nothing
rub my thighs together
spread my green wings and fly

FALL

In the east rain
birds sing deep in their throats
The days sit around
sprouting white hair
but I still go barefoot

WEDDING SONG

My cheekbone floating
on the darkness of her face...

She comes singing like flowers
I reach for her across the water
where I began to walk...

I will be lifted and she will be there...

I KNOW WHAT YOU WANT

Back to the street at
dawn the volcanic darkness
where men fight themselves off
disappears

into bathroom mirrors
amnesia of all that was told
as the proud faces stare from their corners
corner parking lots for the soul grocery stores
gas stations the day restless
as a closing bank

the cemetary cafe serves
breakfast a cup of
flesh gathered in smooth palms
a swollen heart that leaves you
starving between your teeth a wife
who won't let you touch
and a smile topping it off so easy
you don't mind when they hand you the bill

I can't sleep at night
it's hard to turn loose and pull
my eyes from the womb that breathes
its own flesh in steel lungs

one night we were at war

GARY JOHNSON 57

I heard airplanes grinding overhead
their cargo death
my head sick and confused
but it seemed to be what men wanted

that night I dreamed
this spiderweb became a maiden who
held me tenderly in her arms
close to her body I
heard echoes of another life drums
of a black sea
water trickling from my gills

when I awoke
high among stars wings beat
silently to death
someone said you have to
go all the way down to pick it up again

so you and I we
let the maiden stay
you built your city over
her face
her black mouth is open

POEM

Saturday night
in the belly of December
there's a ring around the moon

        "...it's a good omen"

she watches me
take off my socks by the fire

FIRST MOON ACADEMY

When it was all told
the fire to white ash
the house sat back in the black earth

my last friend got up to leave
we walked to his car
put our arms around each other
he crackled off down the narrow road
red lights watching me disappear

the twelfth moon is going down
you can smell it so
mellow like smoldering hay

in a few months
I will dig this stubborn clay
on cool mornings chop
weeds between rows of oakleaf
and pokeweed choking the summer squash

but tonight I give myself to the stars
they hand me their precious gifts
rain drops that will never hit the earth
golden bits of cold sunlight
handfuls of star flesh stark
against my own forgotten meat oils
blood in watering troughs
skin that holds me like a breakfast skillet

the earth turns and faces the north pole
she is naked at last it is wonderful
how she flies back into herself at night

in the house soft whimpers
float like silk from the bed mound
the pot iron stove shudders back to nature
I pull the quilts back and gently
get myself tangled in your warm body
tongues dance around me with news of home
all night I look at the sky

ROBERT L. JONES

Malcolm Huey

I was born in 1943 in Fresno. I grew up and did my public school time
there too. When I finished school I wanted most to be a jazz drummer;
but my hands weren't fast enough so I went to college. After 7 years
(with 2 short periods of living elsewhere: Berkeley and Texas) I got a

BA from Fresno State College, and somehow fell in with the right people. Then I went to Southern California and the University of California at Irvine. I lived in Laguna Beach for 2 years, always close to the ocean, and found some folks there too. In the Summer of 1968 I got married, and finished school the following June. Now I live in Kalamazoo, Michigan, and am a teacher at Western Michigan University. I like it here.

I feel all the time the influence of several poets and poetic people, but I've always hoped that it's been more from their lives than their poems—or their lives through their poems. But my own poems may belie me, so I don't know. Poetry writing is, for me, at the moment, pretty therapeutic, whatever that may mean.

HIS WAKING LIFE

I

To see him sleep, you
wouldn't believe it.
The lip of the sheet

curls at his throat,
breathing with him.
He doesn't move. But

the curtains, as he
has pointed out,
wave goodnight to

someone going under.
Then the air leaves
his mouth in small bursts,

and then his eyes slide
beneath their lids,
describing the old dream.

He said "I wish you'd
be here when one hand
touches the other's palm

and explains what's got
to be done. The face
and the stupid cock

don't give a shit."
He said everything but
what they're after.

He knows the violence
with which his knees drive
into somebody's nuts

but never the sweetness
of the crush that makes
the kneecaps knot

with joy. He wakes,
the ends of his toes blue,
the nails all broken.

II

He holds a photograph.
It is old, scarred.
It could be himself,

it could be anyone,
but he is drawing
it to my face

in his cupped hand.
He is insisting.
Its white edge grows

yellow with the sun
and inward until
it is flame.

And an inch from my face
it is nothing
but a black and printless

hand, blinding me
with his waking life.

AFTERNOON

My mother's first breath was drawn
from the dry heart of afternoon,
and afternoon inhabits every house of her life.
Always the drawers and closets open
to its wooden spoons
and broken garments, its face smiling up
from all the scuffed shoes.
Always the afternoon is filled with the slow
procession through itself.
Always the air holds its memory,
carrying the odors of 50 years of food
and the grease that cooks it,
the odor of rust in the pits of her arms,
odor of her breasts' diminishing
and the blood that hardens within them.

This is afternoon that never gives way to stillness
when she most needs it to be still.
The half-formed gestures go off from her anyway;
they circle around her, describing the body of afternoon.
This is afternoon that never gives way to night
When she most needs to sleep.
It gives light to her small moons of breath,
and to the daily scars of her ankles and hands,
the scar of her belly,
all shining like candles
for afternoon to find its way back.
This is afternoon that doesn't need morning.

It took my mother's place in the womb.
It has taken my place;
it entered, spread itself out
and became the one moment worth two peoples' lives.

ROBERT L. JONES 63

SOMETHING ELSE BEGINS

for Jean

The tongue again slack behind the lips,
the nodding penis,
the fingers emptied of everything upon your body . . .
Each of the senses has groped
along the thread of its history and arrived
at this length of flesh which seeks
only itself
in something that is almost sleep.

Now the edge
extends itself, taking in
you, the bed, everything around me.
Now I rise to a room wholly my own,
lighted only
by the discarded selves
that have gone up in flame throughout the night.

My wish is to gather them up,
the glowing ones, and turn
to those two sleeping bodies so close to death,
to call them awake.

GOING HOME AT NIGHT

I

It must be midnight, or later,
and the moon or a kind street-lamp has sent
a few breaths of light through the closed curtain.
I bend,
and I think I see the lines of her face deepen.
I see the part in her hair
which is the road I've taken, this life
at it's end.

She is a body
of the flesh that has already gone,
making room for the deaths
that cling and haven't done with her yet.

The thing to do is place my mouth
at the dark palm
of the arm outstretched in sleep,
and to feed again.

II

Here is the emptiness, darkened,
and barely lighted by so early a dawn
that the chill is from the inside.
It takes only a moment
for the smile to etch itself,
for things to settle out there around my shoes,
rising up like scuffed gravestones.

Now the hand whose life-line is so like my own
takes mine.
It leads me out and past my body,
into the world that inhabits hers.

Here is her brother, the barber,
looking up from a Tijuana hotel room,
up from a vision of his wife who was everything,
her heart burst on the kitchen floor,
her eyes still holding the dinner she'd made.
We see her death enter him,
fill his body like oil rising
until the light of his eyes flames up
an instant.
We see his hands changed,
the fingers now petals around two buds of air,
two flowers which bloom now
in another world.

Here is the last of her fathers,
his body at rest at the bottom of a river
that flows from his own heart,

his face staring up astonished that it would ever end,
and astonished
that anyone should come to watch it end.

And her mother whose eyes are closed
and at peace,
whose back has grown straight
and might begin again,
whose hair is the color of earth again
and flesh again an orchard,
whose arms go off now
pulling her death along beneath the soil
to the dry edges of Texas.

III

I have gone with her so many times.
I have seen the faces of her beloved dead so many times,
so many times looked into
her face, sleeping and awake, and I know
the dead don't speak to her
and I am so much like the dead.

The room is filling
with the dawn of the next day,
and what is illumined
is a woman,
and around her a family,
of which mine is the last voice.

I know that if when she wakes
she shivers,
it is because my whispers, my false starts,
have passed through an icy throat;
and I know that if she wakes
and asks nothing of me,
it is because her voice too
lies frozen
round the neck of a gravestone.

TEN WINGS

I look down
and I know it is almost over.
They will be ash soon,
the ash that comes from too much water and soap.
They form and reform round what
they've held today.
What else can they do,
short of taking my lapels?

And they wouldn't do that.
No, they are those powerless birds,
the ones who forget,
who fly out a few feet
and go back,
condemned to one tree.
Their ten wings are white
with the white chalk-dust of each word falling.
They couldn't lead me if they wanted to.
They have no friends,
nowhere to go.
I've never introduced them.

ROBERT L. JONES 67

DAVID KHERDIAN

Tom Peck

I was born December 17, 1931 in Racine, Wisconsin, where I lived until the age of nineteen, when I began leaving both voluntarily and involuntarily, until January, 1960, when I left for good. I lived in and around San Francisco from 1960 to 1966, with occasional stays in Fresno. I began writing at the age of 27, but had to put it aside to absorb and pass through the influence of William Saroyan. I didn't start writing again until I had compiled and published *A Bibliography of William Saroyan: 1934-1964* (Roger Beacham, 1965). I then wrote about the San Francisco scene: *Six Poets of the San Francisco Renaissance: Portraits and Checklists* (The Giligia Press, 1967). Second edition retitled *Six San Francisco Poets,* and with new introduction (Giligia, 1969). Then, at the age of 35, I began writing poetry: *Eight Poems* (with Gerald Hausman) (Giligia, 1968); *On the Death of My Father and Other Poems* (Giligia, 1970).

Any biography must be divided into two parts; the years prior to 16, which are unconscious, or consciousness opening, and the years after 16, which are invented. We believe what we say, especially when we write what we claim is the truth. Aside from writing, what I have done since the age of 16 is irrelevant, no matter how damaging it may have been, and supposedly real on that account. It is my early life that concerns me, but it is very nearly impossible to talk about this life, except perhaps as art, because that is the dimension it most nearly approximates. What we know as growing children is instinctive and inseparable from our ecology, because we are controlled then by sun and tides, and our moods are more animal than human. The delicate thread then was not the dichotomy between fantasy and reality, family and solitary wandering, but my own unknowable relation to the sun and plants, and the mysterious upstream movement of fish (that I followed with such rapture and attention as to become Fish myself), that determined the flow and current of my own life. This is the world we forfeit when we acquire adulthood, and this is the world of the unconscious that only children and artists know about. And it is as an artist that I am returning to what was once mine by birthright. Therefore, I have no biography worth telling, as exterior event, and I will not tell that biography until it becomes the equivalent of, and moves parallel to, my own created life, which is poetry. I find in my writing that I gain the future by reclaiming and making whole the past. Only poetry can do this for me, because only through poetry can I achieve a working relationship with my unconscious, which gives shapes and forms to periods lived in chaos and ignorance. It takes years to understand an experience, and a lifetime to know who we are. Therefore, in this true sense, all of my writing is autobiographical, because my own story, when truly told, becomes everyones.

from Homage to Adana

10 YEARS LATER

Standing on the leafy bank
on my first day back;
overlooking hills & ravines
and the river I fished;

I knelt, reached back over
the years, and threw a stick
that tumbled a wild green apple.

One bite and it all came back.

MOVING ALONG DOUGLAS AVENUE

Moving along Douglas Avenue
    late at night
    each night
    shining shoes for
    a dime and a tip
I visit all the bars on State Street
    kneel on sawdust floors;
    loud drunken men; aging
    women that wait and talk
    fondly to a boy.

Finally the Armenian coffee house
    where always one man will
    take a shine and each
    will ask questions to remove
    my embarrassment and their own.
I vow each time will be my last;
    vowed each time my
    life would not be
    lived in these streets.
    this town.

HOWIE AND ME

The ceremony of lines & leaders
    cane poles, buckets,
    stringers & bobbers;
The 8 P.M. appointment with flashlights
    for catching bait—
    nightcrawlers on watered lawns.

The next morning last minute instructions
        from Mr. Sell on where to fish
        & how deep & which holes were best
        for bullheads & cats
Before *he* went off to work and *we*
        went off to Root River, the
        first time alone.

STATE STREET HARRY

He was often on the streets.
        Turning Douglas Avenue on
        the corner of State Street:
        up from the coffee house,
        down from the Serbian bar,
        and near the pool halls,
        where he was most often found
With a cigar jammed in his mouth
        neatly dressed
        seldom speaking but with
        a smile that winked a secret
        he'd never reveal
He was the sharpest pool player
        in town for money;
        an old country bachelor
        from Van
Pushing 50 and maybe older
        but always friendly towards
        those who were learning
        the game; playing us at times
        for no more than the
        cost of a rack;
And sometimes giving tips
        on combinations and english
        that we later used,
And once in back of the Star Restaurant
        late at night
        he stopped a game I was
        ready to concede
        and made a double
        pocket shot I never forgot.

DAVID KHERDIAN 71

ON MILWAUKEE AVENUE

My father always carried a different
look and smell into the house when he
returned from the coffee houses in Racine.
Playing in the streets we would stop,
walk quietly by, and peer in thru the
cracked doors at the hunched backgammon
players, their Turkish cups at their elbows.

Years later, reading the solemn and bittersweet
stories of our Armenian writer in California,
who visited as a paperboy coffee houses in
Fresno, I came to understand that in these
cafes were contained the suffering and
shattered hopes of my orphaned people.

LAKE MICHIGAN'S JOE PERCH

Sun-tanned into wrinkled old age
before his time, he had:
3 cane poles
cat-gut leader
wine bottle corks
and no sinkers on his lines.

Fishing close in on the pier
where the company was select
in water no more than four feet deep
among jagged rocks
where the perch moved easily
in and out,
he eased on and let down
back-hooked minnows
so they wouldn't drown
and at the slightest bite
drifting corks would tilt and run.

In overalls with
minnow bucket
3 cane poles &
hefty stringer

5' 6" Joe Perch
fished among silent imitators,
who seldom complained, and never doubted
that it wasn't luck.

HER PLUM TREE AND SWING

Where was the shelter we
        couldn't find or give
That she sat, back to our
        house and rear window
Motionless in her tree
        swing

And gathered leaves at
        her feet dawn and noon
Autumn and dusk

And waited and told
        the birds and didn't
tell us.

ON MICHIGAN BOULEVARD

On Michigan Boulevard, just up from
        Hamilton Street, on that corner
that is now a playground,
        an old Negro man and his wife
lived in a quiet, empty house
        that was silent
but for the children they
        fed and mothered for brief
moments during the summer
        months.

The old man took me fishing
        once, and fed me once,
and once gave me a nickel.
        And that is all I remember,

DAVID KHERDIAN 73

except for the quiet that surrounded
        him and his wife,
and the ease with which they moved
        and talked and loved.

GENERATIONS AGO

Who were those men
        who sat in the
        sawdust smell
of the woodwork factory
        where Superior Street
        deadends
And ate their lunches
        in the shade of
        those walls
While children all over
        that block
        played & hollered & fought—
Neither noticing the other,
        one grown to middle-age
        the other now dead.

THE CIRCULAR PAVILION

He entered the circular
        pavilion above the lake
        and stepped carefully over
        the weed-controlled cracks
And looked down at the
        empty roller rink,
        deserted pier,
        & fished-washed beach,
And sat on the railing
        returning to the beginning
        of personal time
        and earliest memories
Entering easily into the primal
        waste that he canvassed

with his eyes, thinking how
it was once like this
Hundreds of years before
he was born
but without the artifacts
that he could measure and
let drop with his eyes.

ABOVE THE MOVING RIVER

He saw the gas bubbles as
a boy, staring down
at the river from the city
bridge,
and never guessed that
as he grew into manhood
this river and city—
this very country of
his birth, would fall
into decline and ruin
and total destruction;
that he would have to follow
these factory-spilled
waters beyond the city
limits, and beyond this
state, and then at last
beyond this country,
if he was ever to keep
his boyhood and his
manhood and his children
alive.

PHILIP LEVINE

Tom Peck

Born '28 in Detroit of Jewish immigrant parents. Wayne University. Various Detroit shit jobs. By age of 18 a Red, by 20 dedicated to a poem to explode the nightmare foundries. Education & the frozen fifties helped misplace this pledge. Rejected by Detroit wandered the States, first alone, then with a good woman who became my wife. In '57 came West on writing grant from Stanford. Year of genteel prigs, in loneliness & despair began to write first original poems. Next year came to Fresno in search of hot dry climate for asthmatic son. Found it. Found slowly the brutal landscape & climate which were natural counterparts of streets & shops of Detroit, found friendship, found within the young the voices of poets, found my own poetry, found for as long as it's given a man a home. Before I'd turned 40 kids had helped bring me back to my old Anarchist loyalties. Spent two years in Spain terrified & exhalted before the shrine of Barcelona. Books of poetry: *On the Edge* (Stone Wall Press, 1963), *Not This Pig* (Wesleyan, 1968), 5 *Detroits* (Unicorn Press, 1970), *Thistles* (Turret Books, London, 1970).

RENAMING THE KINGS

River of green stone,
in August '62 I stuck my head in
your lap one mile south of Piedra
where you fall suddenly away
from the highway. 107
in the valley and me
going dizzy, stopped the bike
and stumbled down
over the flat, patient stone, leaned out,
and then you in my eyes,
green tatters of memory, glimpses
of my own blood flashing
like fish, the grasses
dancing calmly, one silver point
like the charmed eye of an eel.
Five hours later I wakened
with the first darkness flowing
from the river bottom
through me to stone, to
the yellow land grasses and storming
the lower branches of the eucalyptus.
I could feel the water
draining from my blood and the stone
going out—the twin bushes of the lungs
held themselves seriously
like people about to take fire,
and when the first minnows startled
I rose into the sky. We

gathered every last tendril
of blue into our breath.

I named the stone John
after my mysterious second born.
High in its banks, slashed with silver,
riding the jagged blade of heaven
down to earth, the river shouts its name.

SATURDAY SWEEPING

Saturday sweeping
with an old broom
counting the strokes
back and forth.
The dust sprays
up silver in the
February sun
and comes down gray.
Soft straw muzzle
poking in and
bringing out
scraps of news,
little fingers
and signatures.
Everybody's
had this room
one time or another
and never thought
to sweep. Outside
the snows stiffen,
the roofs loosen
their last teeth
into the streets.
Outside it's
1952,
Detroit, unburned,
stumbles away
from my window
over the drained roofs

toward the river
to scald its useless
hands. Half
the men in this town
are crying in
the snow, their eyes
blackened like
Chinese soldiers.
The gates are closing
at Dodge Main
and Wyandotte
Chemical; they
must go home
to watch the kids
scrub their brown
faces or grease
cartridges for
the show down.
If anyone knocks
on your door
he'll be
oil flecked or
sea born, he'll
be bringing word
from the people
of the ice drifts
or the great talking dogs
that saved the Jews.
Meanwhile our masters
will come on
television
to ask for our help.
Here, the radiator's
working, stove says,
Don't touch,
and the radio's crying,
I don't get enough.
I'm my keeper,
the only thing
I've got,
sweeping out
my one-room life
while the sun's
still up.

RED DUST

This harpie with dry red curls
talked openly of her husband,
his impotence, his death, the death
of her lover, the birth and death
of her own beauty. She stared
into the mirror next to
our table littered with the wreck
of her appetite and groaned:
Look what you've done to me!
as though only that moment
she'd discovered her own face.
Look, and she shoved the burden
of her ruin on the waiter.

I do not believe in sorrow;
it is not American.
At 8,000 feet the towns
of this blond valley smoke
like the thin pipes of the Chinese,
and I go higher where the air
is clean, thin, and the underside
of light is clearer than the light.
Above the tree line the pines
crowd below like moments of the past
and on above the snow line
the cold underside of my arm,
the half in shadow, sweats with fear
as though it lay along the edge
of revelation.

And so my mind closes around
a square oil can crushed on the road
one morning, startled it was not
the usual cat. If a crow
had come out of the air to choose
its entrails could I have laughed?
If eagles formed now in the
shocked vegetation of my sight
would they be friendly? I can hear
their wings lifting them down, the feathers
tipped with red dust, that dust which
even here I taste, having eaten it
all these years.

THEY FEED THEY LION

Out of burlap sacks, out of bearing butter,
Out of black bean and wet slate bread,
Out of the acids of rage, the candor of tar,
Out of creosote, gasoline, drive shafts, wooden dollies,
They Lion grow.
                    Out of the gray hills
Of industrial barns, out of rain, out of bus ride,
West Virginia to Kiss My Ass, out of buried aunties,
Mothers hardening like pounded stumps, out of stumps,
Out of the bones' need to sharpen and the muscles' to stretch,
They Lion grow.
                    Earth is eating trees, fence posts,
Gutted cars, earth is calling in her little ones,
"Come home, Come home!" From pig balls,
From the ferocity of pig driven to holiness,
From the furred ear and the full jowl come
The repose of the hung belly, from the purpose
They Lion grow.
                    From the sweet glues of the trotters
Come the sweet kinks of the fist, from the full flower
Of the hams the thorax of caves,
From "Bow Down" come "Rise Up,"
Come they Lion from the reeds of shovels,
The grained arm that pulls the hands,
They Lion grow.
                    From my five arms and all my hands,
From all my white sins forgiven, they feed,
From my car passing under the stars,
They Lion, from my children inherit,
From the oak turned to a wall, they Lion,
From they sack and they belly opened
And all that was hidden burning on the oil-stained earth
They feed they Lion and he comes.

THE ANGELS OF DETROIT

I

I could hear them in fever
hovering in the closet or

falling from the mirror. I
could see them in the first dreams
of my dead.
                    Perfume of scorched
clothes . . . she spits back
at the spitting iron, she slaps
it with a round pink palm
and the angels sigh
from the shadowy valleys
of my shirts.

II

I wore angels.
They saved me in the streets
where the towers hung above
suspended on breath, they
saved me from the pale woman
who smoothed the breasts
of chickens or the red-armed
one who sold bread in
the shop of knives.

While I leaned
on the cold stones of summer
and tried to cry and tried
to change they sent me
a robed mother or a
promise in the dark hall.
In the black river at midnight
they said, Go back!

They sent snow
to cover the steps, to crown
the teeth of garbage and bless
the deaths of old cars, snow
falling on our upturned faces
in the great church, the presses
choiring in the roof of night.

III

From Toledo by bus,

from Flat Rock on syphoned gas,
from the iron country on
a dare. For one night.
Stash says, Nigger
boy's crying in
the shit house.

All of us far from
momma and gettin farther.

IV

At the end of mudroad
in the false dawn of the slag heap
the hut of the angel Bernard.
His brothers are factories and
bowling teams, his mother is the
power to blight, his father
moves in all men like a threat,
a closing of hands, an unkept
promise to return.
                        We talk
for years; everything we
say comes to nothing. We drink
bad beer and never lie. From
his bed he pulls fists
of poems and scatters them
like snow. "Children are guilty,"
he whispers, and the soft mouth
puffs like a wound.

He wants it all tonight.
The long hard arms of a black woman,
he wants tenderness, he wants
the power to die in the
chalice of God's tears.

True dawn through the soaped window.
The plastic storm-wrap swallows wind.
'37 Chevie hoodless, black burst
lung of inner tube, pot metal
trees buckling under sheets.
He cries to sleep.

V

In a toilet on Joy Rd
long Eddie on alto.
The yellows of his eyes
brown on pot, the brown centers
burned like washed gold.

Never knew the tune. 16
years old, drummer
had to prod him to music.
So much sorrow in hatred,
so much tenderness
he could taste coming up
from the rich earth.

Little clown. Caught all alone,
arm in a mail-box.
Never did nothing right
except tell the cops to suck
and wave them off like flies.

VI

After midnight of the final
shift, with all our prayers
unanswered, we gave up.
Unvisored pale knot of
West Virginia, mountain rock and
black valley earth, ungloved
yellow potato, dried tubers,
yoked bean, frozen cedars
of weariness, we gave up.

The cranes slip
overhead. The ore pours
from the earth to us, poor earth
somewhere unseamed. If you
listen quiet to Lonnie
next to you or hopping Sugar
you can hear it
piping in pity.

Don't matter what rare breath

puddles in fire on
the foundry floor. The toilets
overflow, the rats dance, the maggots
have it, the worms of money
crack like whips, and
among the angels
we lie down.

VII

Red haired black skinned
Cuban woman. Wait all night
in the parking lot. Doze and talk—
to no one—of home. The panels
of the black chapel flame,
the glass melts or races
with stars. Nothing lasts
forever. Sun up shatters
the yellowed windows of the old Dodge.
She meets us, coatless, in magenta,
an early flower late blooming
in the fenced white wastes,
bare arms open.

LARRY LEVIS

Tom Peck

I was born September 30, 1946, in Selma, California;—actually outside the town, in the country, where my father has a farm. I grew up
there, worked on the farm, and attended public schools in the area.

I read poetry in high school, mainly T.S. Eliot, Frost, Pound, Yeats,
even some Rimbaud and Baudelaire, in English. I didn't understand a
large part of what I read, but if I liked it I didn't really care. When I was
about seventeen I started reading people like Ginsberg, Kerouac's
On The Road, Ferlinghetti and other "Beat" poets—as the magazines
called them then. I was fairly amazed when I found out that Brother
Antoninus was William Everson, who was from Selma. But it wasn't
until I was eighteen and a student of Philip Levine's that I began seriously to write poems at Fresno State College, and later graduated from
there.

I've worked at a lot of different, crazy jobs: on my father's farm, in a cannery, a packing shed, a grocery store in the Sierras, as a helper on a truck, as a porter in a pseudo high class restaurant, and on the yard gang and as a janitor in a steel mill.

At present I am finishing my M.A. degree in Creative Writing at Syracuse University in New York. I am married and happy and writing poems.

MOUNTAINS

It's the silence falling like ashes from the high
meadow that bothers us.

Things want to burst here—
like the slash of the roadside
glaring with shred tires and car sickness,
broken glass and the ripped tongues of shoes.

Even the rocks are troubled
    by a deep itching inside them.

That's why the chain saws whine on like static.
That's why
men breaking for lunch in a clearing
would bite knives.

Above them
all the mountains hold their breath,
    waiting for moths to break free of their stones.

And turning back,
I stop, a dumb fist against a flower.

TRAIN

There is a train I'm on.
It carries scrap iron, the conductor
is hard of hearing,
and has a small dark

hole in the back of his head
that no longer troubles him.

He has a butch hair-cut
cropped so close I can see
underneath where the skin has died,
and is ashes.
We pass by a yard of chickens exploding,
and I try yelling to him
but when he turns
he's all smiles

and trees are slipping past, out
the window,
and small spots of oil under us
like animal droppings or the midnights
you see crossing a face,
as I see them crossing his.

LOS ANGELES AND BEYOND

I

Offshore the ocean
is keeping its hands held under,
It turns now,

while the movie screens go on
dreaming
of bikinis yanked loose and drifting,
of upholstery slashed.

Blown to the gutter
the full color
magazines are spreading like fish tails,
I turn all colors under the neons
like a make-believe,
or a child who can't get his breath.

II

I steal a car and drive softly away.
Leaves stick to the tires for awhile.

POEM

These wings buried beneath a thin cocoon
struggle quietly and open
just as people begin applauding over
by the band-stand.
                  I feel like a
moth on the lip of a waterfall

BAT ANGELS

Sometimes they smear the evening on the air
with wings that
sound like piston slap, just noticed.

In the loose fur
their arm-pits fold like rags,
they leave nose-bleeds on snow, and fall
like hands dropped on shoulders.
       I saw one lift straight up turning to light.

       Sometimes, out for itself,
an angel like this
comes twisting with its dead-pan face
and skitters its blind jaws for meat
over the wind and weeds

It can't be caught, it's mad,
all night it wants
to chew its own blood and whimper and forget
       the flesh it drags—

while the bare rafters tick under the moon.

FISH

The cop holds me up like a fish;
he feels the huge bones
surrounding my eyes,
and he runs a thumb under them,

lifting my eyelids
as if they were
envelopes filled with the night.
Now he turns

my head back and forth, gently,
until I'm so tame and still
I could be a tiny, plastic
skull left on the

dashboard of a junked car.
By now he's so sure of me
he chews gum,
and drops his flashlight to his side;

he could be cleaning a trout
while the pines rise into the darkness,
though tonight trout
are freezing into bits and stars

under the ice. When he lets me go
I feel numb. I feel like
a fish burned by his touch, and turn
and slip into the cold

night rippling with neons,
and the razor blades
of the poor,
and the torn mouths on posters.

Once, I thought even through this
I could go quietly as a star
turning over and over
in the deep truce of its light.

Now I must
go on repeating the last, filthy

words on the lips
of this shrunken head,

shining out of its death in the moon—
until trout surface
with their petrified, round eyes,
and the stars begin moving.

POEM

While the dead jay,
shotgunned and tangled on a wire,
turns over its feathers in wind,

   hands flip through newspapers in town.
And sixty
years from now my skull in the wind,
dug up by a child and jammed on a stick,
for fun.
                    Dirt slips under my heels,
and I step softly out of it all,
like a girl
stepping over her fallen skirts,
or a wheel spinning off an axle,
                  rushing under the moon—

as I open my eyes, blink and hold still.

ROBERT MEZEY

Yasuo Yoshihara

1935: Roosevelt calls for takeover of foreign markets, I am born, and my old man is laid off. The next few years are rather hazy. I remember the heat of the spring sun on my sweater, aged 7, walking down an alley, overturned garbage cans, horribly scarred cats; my country is at war, defending freedom and prosperity. My old man is laid off again. More hazy years. I am in high school, dreaming anguished dreams of unattainable girls and discovering poetry which is to save my life. I have hundreds of pages of Swinburne by heart. My country is at war again, defending freedom and prosperity again. I discover dialectical materialism and lose my faith in God. My old man is laid off again. I go to Kenyon College on a scholarship, flunk out, work in various asylums, warehouses, offices, starve in New York a while, somehow end up joining the army, realizing my first day at Fort Meade that I have made a terrible mistake. I fall in love with an un-attainable girl, go AWOL, go crazy, finally drummed out of army for having years before discovered dialectical materialism. I am 19 years old. At last I get laid. Get married, have baby, go to Iowa City back to school, read classics, write endless poems, drink beer in Ken-ney's, get lost in ego blindness and despair, end of unhappy mar-riage. I live with a succession of attainable girls and write more endless poems mourning the emptiness of the universe. But it's not so bad; I find myself at the beginning of several precious lifelong friendships, I discover grass, and poetry and the love of poetry keep me alive. I try graduate school and promptly drop out in order to keep my love of poetry alive. Get married again, live in Half Moon Bay, Memphis, Fresno and Philadelphia, start teaching, a few months here, a few months there, get fired or unrehired almost everywhere on account of talking too much and growing radical political consciousness. End of second marriage. Return to Fresno, meet Ollie again, former stu-dent, both attainable and unattainable, woman I was looking for all my life, get married third & last time, live in Cleveland, Buffalo, Lan-caster, Philadelphia and elsewhere, still getting fired for teaching Henry Miller and urging draft resistance. Daughter Omi born. Back to Fresno which is becoming home more and more, partly because my two oldest and closest friends live there, partly because I read William Saroyan at age 12 and dreamed of San Joaquin. Son Judah born. I drop acid and discover God. My old man is laid off again. I teach at Fresno State College and begin writing poetry again after two years of silence. Spring of 1968, I get laid off for talking too much, mostly about harmlessness of grass and harmfulness of capitalism and war. Year in mountains, first efforts at communal life, endless stream of new poems, growing awareness of distance between radical consci-ousness and my own life, inner & outer. Troubles and discoveries. Many books coming out, new poems and anthologies, but very little money coming in. Beginning to grow old but still a kid from Philadel-phia at heart, and much happier than in youth, also unhappier. The planet is poisoned, the human heart is poisoned, but the universe is still as always a perfect flower. Poetry teaches me patience and joy. We must learn to face death, which will come soon. It is 1970.

IN THIS LIFE

Now the cup of grasses and down is cool,
the eggs cool, the throne empty
from which she would step down and growing still,
look out long toward the darkness.

One moist and terrible night, it came creeping
and tensing its jaws and it too grew still
and then it had her,
and a small diamond of light opened in her brain.

I remember the eyes closed tight
against the final ecstacy of the teeth,
the weightless blood-beaded lump of feathers buried now
under the iris slowly eaten alive by the air.

Here is the father
blossoming on a twig
to sing the song of the bleeding throat
on this day of crystal wind and young sunlight.

He sings the endless song
of irises wrinkling and wrinkling and becoming nothing,
road of fine sand strewn with fallen wings,
the mouse, the toad, the blind nestling taken in deep grass,

he sings of a diamond, sings
of the spokes flashing brilliance at the center
of the ceaselessly collapsing floor of bone
and I wish I sang with him,

he sings the only truth
in this world where men remember mostly lies,
sings it and sings it
till it breaks at last into particles of light,

blossoms of mercy
in the midst of the holocaust.

LAST WORDS

To John Lawrence Simpson, 1896-1969

Like men who meet
for the first time from opposite ends of the earth,
we never talked much.
You sat
at the kitchen table, in a chair
only the smallest children dared to sit in,
yelling at your sons or telling some sly story,
or silent, looking out the window
at the cows ambling toward the low sun,
and I sat next to you
with my hands folded,
staring at your daughter, barely listening,
a writer of books, a poet.

Now what was faithful
most of a century to the earth
and the darkness of the earth
is preparing to become the earth,
and what was faithful to the light
is turning painfully into light.
Now I want to say
what I have never said.

Old man, sometimes I felt like a child
sitting next to you.
I watched your hands
that were strong and twisted as roots pulled from the earth
and the blue smoke curling upward in the silence
and felt like a child.

There were many things I did not understand.
How easily fooled I was
by your fierceness, your long silences,
your rants against communism.
How easily I assumed
your distaste for my long hair and my long face
and my long history of childhood.
Still, I listened to your stories

and I remember well
the mules straining in the darkness, bitter thin air,
the mountain road covered with snow, the huge logs
covered with snow,
and summer nights in the old days,
wild girls riding bareback over the foothills,
sisters of rustlers, going to a dance,
and the old Indian
hitting a big hole and going down thrashing and burning
in the gravel,
and I remember what I saw,
long after midnight in the cold shed,
the long rip in the cow's side,
the silent man with his arm
plunged in up to his shoulder, the cow's head
secured in the iron stanchions, her eyes
black and enormous with agony,
the cloud of her breath, the cloud of mine,
no sound, blood everywhere,
I remember what I saw in your eyes.

And I see
drifting through the smoke and fog
the cool sun—
through the wreckage of years, cars,
dead pigeons, dead wives,
good deals and foolish charity,
money made and lost,
made again and lost again,
a dead baby, a dead son growing rich in the east,
the leaves dying on the vine,
the dying sun,
through death and divorce and dull disaster
a young and tender spirit.

The road is paved,
the hole filled in,
the girls lie under the stones
of Academy Cemetery
many years.
The old mountain men
are gone for good into the mountains,
the sound of their laughter growing very faint
and the wind keeps blowing.

96 ROBERT MEZEY

KALEIDOSCOPE

Everywhere man is born free
and everywhere he is in chains
I remember reading that
And laugh bitterly but we are no different

Ideas surround me with spears
And certain images
Climb up before dawn and bang at the silence
Instruments of torture

Black armbands converging on all the roads
A sudden flash of teeth deep in the sea
And there is a glass tear shining
On the helmets of the police

My sight descends into the blackness
That begins at the muzzle and gets deeper
No end no end to the blackness
Of that implacable hole

The flag of my country
Freshly laundered whips in the breeze
It is a beautiful morning
A man is beaten to death under the County Jail

I have been up all night
Toying with words
And hiding my face in my hands
I walked outside

The stars set so slowly
In a few minutes they were gone
And there was nothing nothing at all
In the pale blue sky

POEM

Stars overhead
A frog's grunt from the other side of the pond
Clear sound in the summer night

Ollie is asleep
My warm foxy girls
Curled up at my sides
In my lap the story of a king and his youngest daughter

The perfume of hair
Little Omi is breathing the pure breath of sleep

Eve moves to the open door
My senses are full
Of her slim young womanly body
and tinkling anklets

I am ready for sleep

Orion blows like a kite in the summer sky
I think I will climb up his tail
To freedom

HERE

I want to speak to you while I can,
in your fourth year before you can well understand,
before this river
white and remorseless carries me away.

You asked me to tell you about death.
I said nothing. I said

This is your father,
this is your father like water,
like fate,
like a feather circling down.

And I am my own daughter
swimming out,
a phosphoresence on the dark face of the surf.

A boat circling on the darkness.

2

She opens her eyes under water. The sun climbs.
She runs, she decapitates flowers.
The grass sparkles. Her little brother laughs.
She serves meals to friends no one has seen.
She races her tricycle in circles.
I come home. The sun falls.

3

You eat all day.
You want to be big. "Look how big!"
you cry,
stretching your arms to heaven,
your eyes stretched
by all the half terrified joy of being in motion.

The big move clumsily, little love,
as far as I can see.
They break everything
and then they break,
and a pool of decayed light sinks back into the earth.

Writing these words tonight,
I am coming to the end
of my 35th year. It means nothing to you
but I rejoice and I am terrified
and I feel something I can never describe.
They are so much the same,
so much the sun blazing on the edge of a knife...

We are little children
and my face has already entered the mist.

4

I hear you cry out
in the blackened theatre of night.
I go in and hold you in my arms
and rock you, watching
your lips working,

your closed eyelids bulge with the nightly vision.

At last you grow quiet
and the old cricket silence
gathers again.
The squirrel—the squerlu
is only a stain,
a something dark on the highway
where the flat fur
barked its skin to the wind till it blew away,
and you are still
chewing the mystery,
losing yourself once more
in the single, cold, unbreakable
fact.

5

I get lost too, Naomi,
in a forest that suddenly rises
from behind my breastbone on a night of no moon.
Stars hang in the black branches,
great, small,
glittering like insoluble crimes,
ceaselessly calling me
toward that thick darkness under the trees.
I turn, sobbing, to run,
but it is everywhere.

6

I wanted to give you something
but always give you something else.
What do you call it when it is underground
like a cold spring in the blood,
when it is a poem written out of naked fear
and love which is never enough,
when it is my face, Naomi,
my face
from which the darkness streams forth?

The petal falls,
the skin crumbles into dirt,
consciousness likewise crumbles
and this is one road the squirrel will not cross again.

I was here, Naomi,

I will never be back
but I was here,
I was here with you and your brother.

AT LAST

Now darkness rains down
On the hard ground scraped from the eyes of heaven
Swirls in the rising and falling fields
Looking for its children
This is the first night of the journey
Night of wind
Touching the clean black steel of autumn
Flowers cut down and curled into wisps of ash
Night of silence
Where you are going

No more tears
All the living
That weep looking down at the door of the world
Have climbed into their cars and disappeared
And you are alone with your death
At last

KHATCHIK MINASIAN

I was born in Fresno, California on the 2nd of August, 1913 and immediately named Khatchik after my grandfather who perished in Armenia, 1897. My father died when I was five and I went to work a few years later in a neighborhood bakery for three loaves of bread a day. Four years later, I was in the vineyards as a grape picker, field hand, box maker, car loader, truck driver, and a host of other field exercises. My strength and nourishment came thru day-dreams, and from my cousin, William Saroyan, who supplied me with strength, humor, companionship and understanding. When I was 15, during a spring rain, a sky full of fantasy descended into which I escaped at will—the world of poetry.

I attended Fresno State College from 1932-34, and began a poetry column in the Hairenik Weekly which ran through the thirties and forties. From the very beginning, however, there were setbacks. Every time I wrote a poem and foolishly made this announcement, I was chased out of the house with curses by my maternal grandmother, for wasting good time that could have been spent brooming out someone's doorway, and always accompanied by a screeching reminder that one writer in the family was enough.

When word reached me that I had won the 1945 Edwin Markham Gold Medal Award for poetry, we were excited and made guesses as to its size and shape and weight. My brother Kirk said two feet, I said four, Bill said ten, and we all laughed; all in jest, of course. For days we looked eagerly for a truck to turn up our street. What other conveyance could manage such an award in gold. We watched and waited, and through the mail came a small package, the award, no larger than a silver dollar, but beautifully engraved and designed. The more I studied the award, the larger it became.

We moved to San Francisco in 1935. Published *Grief's Exile; a Tragedy in Four Acts* (The Pyramid Press, 1940), *Bells and Sermons* (The Lutheran Literary Board, 1940), *A World of Questions and Things* (The Decker Press, 1950), and *The Simple Songs of Khatchik Minasian* (The Colt Press, 1950 and The Giligia Press, 1969). I married Helen Feigert, February 22, 1947. Moved to Palo Alto, where I reside, a father of six children.

VALLEY DITCH

In our ditch
    there are water skaters,
    frogs,
    tall reeds,
    mud bugs,
    apple cores and plum seeds,

    and little naked children.

RULE 449

boy with blackspider
on hat,
and four June bugs
on new red sweater,
parades before student body
holding bull-frog high.

principal summons boy
to office,
begins with rule 173—
(not to molest fellow student)
                            eye on spider;
ends with rule 449—
(becomes property of school)
                            hand on bull-frog.

AN EVENING AT HOME

The guests are seated in the evening parlor
smoking Izmir tobacco;
they are pleased.
The children will have dried figs
and candied nuts.
Suddenly a guest is praised for her gifted voice,
dragged to the piano
by the bearded aunt,
giggles and cannot sing.
Excitement wears to silence.

The hostess serves coffee
in the new gift cups;
the parlor becomes a tavern,
there is smoke and noise,
the sleepy children are bored,
they drift to various rooms.

The guests must go,
the children nod and fret,
and then commotion in the house
as hat and wrapper hunts begin;
farewells are shouted and exchanged,
but wait! the guests will take dried figs
and candied nuts with them.

Another pause, another word or two,
another dip of Izmir for the pipes.

They go at last,
they know the way.

THE HOLY WAR

We go to the meadow,
    a small army.
We are going to gather mushrooms
    and firewood.
We carry spade and axe
    and gunny sacks.

Nothing will stop us.

OCEAN EPISODE

From the roof the rain tumbles
in throbs
and circles away
to the low spot in our yard.
I watch the lake widen to the barn,
disturbing the walnuts
I had spread to dry.

Now like a house boat
half submerged,
our barn stands in the lake,
and from an opening
the walnuts float outside,
like sailors fleeing from their sinking craft.
Then spin and bob
and rush and roll
they fall into the rushing of the over-flow
and hurry to the ocean
forming in the empty lot.

I look to the empty lot,
to the dark forms moving about,
perhaps the neighbors;
I watch them rescuing the sailors
in their gunny sacks.

OLD THINGS

These are old leaves,
    do not disturb them.

The wind is shaking olives down.

These are old thoughts,
    do not destroy them.

She is wearing out my heart.

THE TIGER WIND

The wind,
playing in the violets,
sprang upon me.

Oh! I thought,
if I could be so familiar
with her.

THE UNFORTUNATE

In my garden
    there are butterflies.

I gather them
    to preserve their beauty.

O unfortunate women! I think.

THE CURE

Restless
I pace my little room,
swing the windows and look out.

The trees on the hill are tossing madly;
I watch them,
I am thrilled at their madness.

I turn to my bare room satisfied.

BEYOND THE GAGE

We probed the universe
on the heights of Aragats,
made positive identifications
in the light-year zone,
viewed Uranus calmly
as if a tempting plum
just overhead,
closed the session smartly with a gay huzzah
and started down the heights
when suddenly a wall of hieroglyphics
tumbled out of the centuries
and confounded us all.

DeWAYNE RAIL

Tom Peck

I was born in Round Prairie, Oklahoma, on September 29, 1944. I was seven when my family moved to Fresno, in 1952, in search of money and happiness. But we found neither. We had given up being poor farmers to become poor laborers, and for the next three or four years we worked in the cotton fields, peach orchards, and vineyards around Fresno, in the hopeful way that poor people sometimes have, to save money. We saved enough money to return to Oklahoma and fail at farming in 1956. We spent a long summer working in Fresno, and we saved enough money to return to Oklahoma and fail at farming again in 1957. Finally, we settled in Fresno with that feeling of perpetual discontent that has plagued all the members of my family ever since.

At Roosevelt High School and at Fresno State College, I became educated and learned that I was cut out for bigger and better things than farm labor. So I became a janitor. And a night-watchman, a saw operator in a box factory, a lidding machine operator in a packing house, a bus-boy in a gourmet restaurant, and a clerk at a drive-in dairy.

I began to write poems. For most of my life I had thought of myself as a writer, had even hinted to a few friends that I was going to be one, although I had never written very much. But at Fresno State, I began to try to write. I picked up a book of poems, *The Less Deceived* by Philip Larkin, and that turned the trick. I was so excited by his poetry that I began to make up poems, and I began to take writing classes, first from Peter Everwine and then from Philip Levine. I was so excited that I managed to finish college in six years instead of the ten I had planned on. I was excited enough to go away to graduate school and waste two years learning things about poetry that I didn't even want to know. I got an M.F.A. and of course I became a teacher.

I teach composition now at Valley College in San Bernardino. I am happily married, and my wife, Maria, and I are planning on a vacation in Greece and a house with a couple of acres somewhere near Fresno.

THE IDIOT

He would plow barefoot behind a mule
in a field at the edge of town,
the town kids said.

I remember how they took me there
my first day after school, to show me,
and pestered him with questions:

Who cut your hair, Carl?
Do you sleep here?
Don't you ever wear shoes?

He didn't get mad.
He gave us some
ripe tomatoes from his patch

and stood grinning while we ate them,
glad we were there,
knee-deep in vegetables and kids.

THE FIELD

This field is the last refuge of squirrels,
jackrabbits, and mice. Deserted, left
to its own devices, it has taken years
to grow a thick cover of weeds that tangle

And arch over long tunnels. A dozen
kinds of birds feed here on sprays of seeds
that hang from dried stalks, and tracks lead
everywhere. At dark, the animals push up

From their holes and look cautiously out.
The hours between now and dawn belong to them.
They sniff the air, or nibble
at young shoots of grass, and each one moves

Slowly away from his den. They are free
to wander the length of the field,
never hunted, as each night rolls
easily into the next. Some stay on here

For years. Others die, drawn
to the highway that loops the edge of the field,
with its hiss of cars whose headlights
shine briefly into their lives, then flash on.

THE GARDENER

Each morning
the old man
staggers down the steps
to his flower garden
where he busies himself
at planting seeds,
watering,
or fiercely potting plants.

He moves like a cold insect
among the flowers
before the sun rises
to warm his legs and arms.

He makes his way
carefully
around the space he has
cleared for himself
away from the streets and the cars:
in and out
of the tool shed,
sharpening things,
trading a hoe
for a spade or pruning shears.

He works his plot of ground
as though he could bring
the soil to life,
kneading it,
combing it until
it breathes easily
around the roots of plants,
clearing it of stones,
occasional sticks,
and stubborn
clumps of dirt
which he crumbles in his hands
and scatters
like the ashes of the dead.

GOING HOME AGAIN/POEM FOR MY FATHER

Nothing here seems to welcome my return,
the dark and weeded fields, those dying trees.
Walking this ground, I see how things have turned.

Ten years ago I played here in this yard.
With sticks for mules, I mimicked every move
my father made behind that rusting plow.

And nights when he came home too tired to move,
he sat upon that stoop and slowly cursed
the land, the lack of rain, his crops, his luck.

I grew up on this farm and learned to curse
what made him hang on to his father's place,
the bank that threatened to foreclose each year,

The wind, this house and land, and his plodding ways
that kept us here, losing, year after year.
How much it marked him. Indeed, my father's face

I can still see, grown old as dirt, the lines
like furrows in the stubble of his face.

HOUSE

I remember the great rooms
with no ceilings, and the way
the rafters disappeared up
into the darkness over my head.
A kerosene lamp would throw
just enough light to keep
me scared. And I would magnify
every little sound the house
made at night in the wind.

I recall the last winter
we spent there, snowed in,
on the edge of the prairie.

112 DeWAYNE RAIL

Nothing could stay warm.
I would curl up in bed
like a squirrel, and lie awake,
listening, while the fire
died out, and the old beams
cracked like bones overhead.

PANTHER CREEK

I

Leaf drifts have choked the trail
for a hundred yards on this side of the creek,
and today I walk through them,
knee-deep in the damp mould.
Ahead, I see the sloping bank
and the brush that grows thick there.
I can see vines, tangled, and thick as rope,
that swing over the one deep pool in Panther Creek.

Ten years have killed the oak that grew
by the stream's edge,
that dwarfed the blackjack and hickory.
It lies half-in the water,
shedding scabs of bark.

Downstream, a tangle of snags
Backs water at the old fording place.

II

It was in these shallows that
        I used to play.
All summer once I stayed
        here every day
while my father plowed across
        the bottomland.

Alone, I ranged these banks,
        fishing for cat,
or making dams of sand

and long networks
of shallow pools as traps
        for tiny perch.

Slowly, I guided each
        one to the pools.
Then, rifling the water, I
        would make them move
by chasing them with sticks
        and shading them

Until they stopped. Calmed,
        they nibbled at
my hands until I placed
        them in the creek,
or slapped them out to die
        among the leaves.

III

Somewhere a hawk screams,
and I can feel the sudden hush of sound.

A dry leaf rattles in the wind.

Nervous, I squat in the shade of a bush
and trace a set of small, bunched tracks
that lead toward the creek.

I wait for the coming back of sound,
the wrangling of birds, and squirrel-chatter—
noises I can recognize.

Even the creek seems quieter than I remembered,
the water darker somehow,
with a slow, insistent push.

IV

Early, the shadows deepen on the sandy bottom.
I rise, and from where I stand I can see only

the dark surface of the creek,
and my footprints slowly filling with water
where I knelt in the damp sand to drink.

PICKERS

Scattered out like a handful of seeds across
The field, backs humped to the wind,
Faces like clumps of dirt in the white rows,
Their hands keep on eating cotton.
The long sacks fill and puff up tight,
Like dreams of money they're going to make
Or of what they'll have for supper.
They stagger with the weight to the wagon and scales,
Dragging their tracks out in the dust,
Faces bent close to the ground,
Their hands ragged from the cotton bolls.

TULSA

I got off the freight one night
In Tulsa, years back. Broke, and young,
I knocked at palace doors and begged
For food, and shivered until dawn.

Fifteen hundred miles from home,
And walking hungry through that town,
I heard far-off oil wells pump,
Like rich, soft laughter, on and on.

DENNIS SALEH

Tom Peck

I suppose I am something like an Anglo-Egyptian; my father's parents came to Fresno from Egypt, one Elia and one Saleh, and my mother's maiden name was McKoy. My father was born in Fresno, left for some years, and returned to go into business as a painting contractor in 1948. I was born in Chicago in 1942 and raised in Fresno from 1948 on.

I attended Fresno State College, the University of Arizona, and the University of California, Irvine, where I received a Master of Fine Arts Degree in creative writing. I taught one year at U.C. Riverside and am teaching now at U.C. Santa Cruz. The most interesting job I ever had was working for Mid-Tower Publishers in Fresno, when their *Sex*

Life of a Cop was in flower, and when Fresno was called by at least one crusader "the smut capital of the world."

One of the few things I have to say about poetry is to acknowledge the great debt I owe to Philip Levine. He helped me not take my writing seriously when that was important, and when the time came, was the first to suggest I ought to take it seriously. At the moment I'm working on two books, a collection of my own poems, and a book called *just what the country needs Another Poetry Anthology.*

A GUIDE TO FAMILIAR AMERICAN INCEST

THE MOTHER

wished to have been milk,
to have passed out of herself entirely,
to have passed out of her nipple.

She searches through herself
for the devil's mark,
the place her son can enter
and not be felt.

Oh if she finds it

THE SON

behaves peculiarly,
as if sensing what will fall
to him to do.

If he stands at a window,
he tastes it. His tongue reaches out
hesitantly to touch the glass,
half expecting to press through it
to nothing.

When he passes them,
he is afraid he will press
through his mother,
press through his sister.

He watches his father as though
watching a manta ray
approach him from a closet.

THE DAUGHTER

lingers in the bathroom.

She stands on the scale
and imagines how the years
will touch her here, and so,
delicately, like a towel.

Her breath is short, heavy,
a whisper that grows between her legs
like grass to be cut
late in the morning, when dry.

THE FATHER

Everything he says catches
in the air before him,
is a pale and wobbly reflection
nodding gently from his mouth.

He follows it from room to room,
and it crosses and re-crosses
the balloons he sees in everything,
the tense balls of promise.

The father is nothing exacting,
only the suggestion of water moving
through water, parting water.

THE PENIS

It should be porcelain
and harmless. Or we should
be able to warm our hands at it.
It could warm our hearts.

It will make the air in the room
ring like a bell
and it will beat for an answer.

THE THUMB

To end it all, the people elected a thumb.

It stood before them blankly,
as a thumb would.

Its nail flickered and blinked
in the fires people put at its feet
at night.

The people would sit with it,
holding each other, rocking.

It was strange.

What was the meaning of the cloud
joined neatly to the cuticle.
What was the cuticle doing.

Like a leader,
the thumb stood in mystery.

And what did it do? What could it do.
It pressed.

Like an iron, a tack,
like the pages of a book coming together
for the last time.

FRANKENSTEIN'S JOURNAL

As if they had wills—
five wills of their own,
the fingers refuse to move.
How can I go further?

Tonight four new hands were brought to me.
They look good. I am particularly happy
with the pink still in the nails.
I have determined an answer to the fingers.

***

The castle presents its problems.
The damp.
There is nothing to be done with the
porcelain; the stains will not come out.

***

January seventeenth.
Is it not appropriate? That
the eyes arrive this week?

***

. . . *but the power of regeneration*
is still possessed to a great degree,
though diminished because
of the greater specialization
of cells in the earthworm's body.

If an earthworm is cut in two
between segments 15 and 18,
the head piece will regenerate
a new tail and the tail piece,
a new head.

***

Last night I dreamed
of the great black bird
tattooed on its chest.
Its two parts fluttered apart
and I could see myself
sewing the bird together.
It is curious that I should
dream of the tattoo only.

***

The creature quite...
Pleases me?
I would have liked it
to have had more hair.
A larger nose.

***

Dawn clears across the face of the body.
What does not clear
is this return to the old problems,
this slow spill of wax worked to work at light,
the candle's nightmare at the dawn.
Is it a worm story then, my work?
And at this end, worm, what are we?

***

April: Electricity!

***

One could smell the sea close at hand tonight.
What great clouds of dead fish
there might have been overhead.
I wonder if my work is not finally
some great marine venture.
What would the early ocean say to me tonight?
Would it mark the pretense of so many cells?
That I should tease their quick?

***

Frankenstein, Frankenstein...

***

God that it is an *it*!

***

I am so afraid—
now that I may be right.
There's something in the body.

***

LUIS OMAR SALINAS

Tom Peck

Luis Omar Salinas   born 1937
Robstown, Texas
Employed: F.S.C.

I am Omar the Crazy Gypsy
I genuflect in church when the priests are not looking and hold hands
with the devil when I can.
   My past is the rendition of an opera, sad faced, muddy hands, open
eyed. The villain is dead I killed him. I know how to love and exist.
Whitman's America is not dead; and when the time comes, I will be
there to shake hands with his grandmother passing out leaflets against
the war and when my mind heals solid like a rock, I will throw my
arms up and exclaim: I'm a Mexican...damn it, damn it can't you
understand MEXICAN.

from Crazy Gypsy

I

I am Omar
  the crazy gypsy
    nimble footed
    and carefree

  I write poems
    on walls
      that crumble
      and fall

  I talk to shadows
    that sleep
    and go away
      crying

I meet fearless girls
    who tell me
      their troubles
        my loneliness
          bottled up in their
            tummy.

III

My spine shakes
        to the songs
        of women

    I am heartless and lonely
        and I whistle a tune
            out of one of my dreams
                where the world
                    babbles out loud
                        and Mexican hat check girls
                        do the Salinas Shuffle
                        a dance composed
                        by me in one
                            of my nightmares
                            and sold
                            for a bottle
                                of tequila.

IV

I am Omar
    the crazy gypsy
        I waltz through avenues
                of roses
        to the song
                of Mariachis

V

I am Omar
    the Mexican gypsy
. . .
        I speak of love
            as something
        whimsical and aloof
            as something
        naked and cruel

124 LUIS OMAR SALINAS

I speak of death
as something inhabiting
the sea
awkward and removed

I speak of hate
as something
nibbling my ear . . .

VI

I am Omar

. . . the eyes of Guevara
are wandering
through the grape orchards
of California

brothers in "barrios"
breathe the air
of revolution

NIGHTS AND DAY

I am alone
and with me
the roads
as empty containers

if you become
saddened
by suffering
butterflies

Look to the right
and you see a town
on the other side
where the neighbors
hide themselves

like a swallow
working in hell
for low pay

I could have
imagined this
a world before
but not this
night of darkness

not this night

THROUGH THE HILLS OF SPAIN

for Miguel Hernandez

Through the hills of Spain
among the flowers and the seeds of life
a train wanders

Hernandez... Hernandez

the night is hushed
mockingbirds listen
to the tirades of men
wounded in battle

blood of your blood
senseless death in the air
the wind swallows birds

Hernandez... Hernandez

There is death caught by the nostrils of the sky
there is death everywhere
the sea calling to forlorn travelers

Hernandez... Hernandez
your wound leaves the redness of skies never conquered
untouched, virginal

Oh, yawning tenderness
lust on the wheels of a train

blood on the faces of bulls
soil calloused by murder
homicide of undertakers
and children

Sword of the flesh   Alicante
ripe years of manhood
Oh, dawning life
overpowering weatherworn axes
heaven of your life

Hernandez. . . Hernandez

Through the hills of Spain
among the flowers and the seeds of life
a train wanders

SATURDAY

It is Saturday. . . day of apples and turnips
on heavy trucks that pass my aunt's house
sleeping. My cousin is awake quibbling with
his painful back, this corner of the earth
surrenders to the anarchy of cows.

We are off to see the movies and the flesh of
night is torn into small, little children
as angels eat breaded clouds and spiders
tell stories to the rabbits of the neighborhood.

SUNDAY. . . . DIG THE EMPTY SOUNDS

It is Sunday and I look for you
a meteor, wandering, lazy,
simple as dust. I've encountered life here
a single shadow discovering the breast.
I bake the joys of afternoons in the sun,
with the blood of children
running weakly through the street
struck dumb by dark.

The human eyes of women loiter
here like stars on the cobblestones
water of the oppressed
standing still on the horizon
caught like a fish in the narrow heart
of mice . . .

The human mouths of clouds
go by here
running thieves in the sunlight.

I survive the rain
dreaming, lost, frowning
the shoes of my mother
talking
to the children in Africa
to the crazy dogs
that huddle in corners
starving
empty of sound.

LA CASA DE MI AMIGO

    for Phil

En la casa
voces y muchachos.

. . . a woman
   a poet
   a dog
   and Spanish
clouds.

It is the home
of my friend
let's listen.

PEDRO

(Pedro Infante—Mexican Singer, Actor, Genius who died pilot-
ing his own plane, April, 1957 at the age of 37)

You took the world and embraced
  it as a child
    your arms   your voice   your heart
        touched the sea

    you had many loves
        among them Mexico

when you died
        it rose to its feet
        to pay homage to you

mountains of snow
        were singing your songs

Pedro I remember you
        when I was a child
        and how you brought
                tears

    silence within silence

ARAM HAPPY MONEY MAN

You chew the apples of yesterdays encampment
and sit like the Budda
        unknown
    the seeds of winds
    instill in you a sacred beauty
    and we know you as a friend.

LUIS OMAR SALINAS 129

HERBERT SCOTT

Born in Norman, Oklahoma in 1931. Married, a year after graduating from high school in University City, Missouri. Have worked as a grave-digger, farm hand, factory worker, grocery and produce clerk, near Chicago, and in Oklahoma and California. Children one, two, three, and four came along while I worked 70 hours a week for Safeway Stores in Oklahoma (no union). Finally loaded up the old Chevy, latter-day Okies, the baby in a cantaloupe crate in the back seat, and headed for California and a 40 hour work week. Same supermarket chain, fewer hours, more money. All that wealth and free time, en-rolled at Fresno State College in 1960, and graduated in 1964. Attend-ed the University of Iowa on a fellowship, assistantship, and a job in a printing plant. In two years added child number five and an M.F.A., in that order. I am now living in Kalamazoo with the same wife (Diane), and the same five children (Herbert, Megan, Rannah, Erin, Kyla), and teaching creative writing at Western Michigan University, where I am an assistant professor in the English Department.

LATE FALL, SETTING TRAPS

I climb like a fever to the forest.
Coyotes creep by my fingers,
possum hang on by breath.

I enter the tongue of a fox,
the oneness of bees,
my mouth puckering
in persimmon whistles.

Beyond the perimeter of motion
ears blame me into silence,
mistletoe gathers the tops of trees.

I set my traps, the creek
freezing at my step.
I won't catch it next Spring
when it gallops like deer down its track.

PASSING THE MASONIC HOME FOR THE AGED

Winter has come to the old folks' home.
The summer chairs on the porch
are facing the wall, bending
in prayer. Snow hangs

like a shawl across their backs.
On the lawn, drifts grow like weeds,
and the branches of trees snap
at one another. The street

has gone away to stay.
Under a roof heavy with clouds, screens creak
like old bones. Inside, the faces
of ten thousand winters press the panes.

THE MAN IN THE CLOSET

He tried living in a closet
and the closet loved him
and held all his dreams
for him to see,
with the broom smelling
of Mexican factory workers,
and wine fields from the broken jug,
and the raincoat he never wore
feeling like the oilcloth table cloth
in the tenant house with red mud at the door.

He lived in the closet
fondling papers from the shelf,
having meals brought
by hitting his head against the door,
relieving himself through the keyhole,
but giving that up and using
a chipped enamelled pot,
with a strainer, in case something
precious had been taken and passed.

SPRING COMMENCES

It is like winter
although the children wade
in mud ponds
and flowers float like birds
across the field.
Winter has been here.
One can see that. Your face
is of winter. I noticed this
before, in that landscape,
after the deep snow,
reflections of coldness,
of clear sky,
before the earth broke through.
The coldness remains
although your hand
turns the fresh soil

and insects disembark
like explorers from canoes
to search the dark land.

EXCAVATIONS

Centuries have passed
since these fires burned in other faces.
Was there dancing, then, love-making,
lean children in the huts,
deer grazing at the edge of the clearing?
Were there antelope hides curing in the wind,
then, pungent and beautiful,
before the earth rose and gathered them, all?
These drawings on the cliff enlighten us.
We notice here their separation from the tribe,
a cruel winter flight across high mountains.
And here, the murder of a chief, much-beloved,
the sacrificial burning of his wife.

What do we hope to learn?
We spend our summers here, and bring our wives.
There was no great civilization,
no monumental work. They came here, lived,
grew sick, and died. They fed on venison
and squirrel, and laid their beds on poplar leaves.
They bound their feet when winter came,
and built the snow to keep the wind away.
And what decisions did they make?
Where did they miscalculate?
We come with shovels and with sieves
and pan for bones, small hunks of clay, bright beads.

But as we dig we talk of death,
of bodies settling in the ash
of their own fire. And in our tents at night
we gather what we have, of what we are,
our bodies, breath, whatever clings,
and learn to wage a kind of love.
The summer wears, the bones collect,
the nights grow cold; we try to resurrect
something from the ashes that we hold.

THE APPRENTICE GRAVE DIGGER

"You'll always have a job."

1.

There is a place for every body:
the Rich, the Black,
the Paupers, and the Masons.

The Rich have frontage on the road;
the Masons sleep together in neat rows;
the Black lean back in weeds,
beyond the grass, where spotted
ground squirrels burrow in their holes.

2.

Three feet of dirt
and two of clay,
the last, grey slate
that's hard to chip away.

We dig them clean and straight
as if our lives depended on it.

3.

The mourners come,
a fluttering of clothes,
in loose formations
through the stones

like birds that search
for scattered seed
on wintered fields.

4.

Two buddies
roared their bikes
beneath a cement mixer
and mixed their bodies.
No telling who

was where or what.
They dug out.
I dug them in.

5.

Six months and three hard rains
the boxes go,
the earth caves in.

Wood roots as good
as man, I think

The ground now knows
its tenant, not by
reputation.

We truck dirt in
and fill the graves again.

6.

T. C., Red, and Boomer
pushed me in a grave
and cranked the casket down
till I was flat, stretched out,
my hands above my chest.

"White boy's learning
how to die,"
they laughed and cried,
then pulled me out
and washed my head.

7.

We dug one up instead of down.
The widow came to supervise
the moving to a larger plot.
We winched him high, the vault,
expensive moisture-proof cement,
had split. He tipped

and poured himself a drink.

She knew him right enough.
He rained a putrefaction
you could keep.

8.

Each time
the same sad words
for stranger bodies,

women cold with fear,
children weeding noses,

husbands wheezing
rumors of death.

9.

I killed a king snake sunning
in the branches of a cedar,
cut him with a spade
until he spilled
his breakfast on the grass.

Five sparrow babies,
slick and sweet,
poured out like heavy jam,
the fruit still warm.

I nudged them in the grave.
The snake, the birds, the man,
together in the ground.

10.

When it rains
we bury ourselves
in piles of plastic grass,

in the shed,
with straps and shovels,
and visions of the dead.

11.

I don't like to dig
the children's graves.
They cramp you in,
not room enough
to swing your axe
or work a sweat.

I'd like to climb in,
brace my back,
and push them longer.
If I was stronger.

12.

"What do you do?"

I build holes in the ground.

PICTURE PUZZLE

This piece of sky goes somewhere
above the child's head, the child
with the apple—the sky is blue here,
no clouds in this part of the picture.
But first we must find the child's head.
It is somewhere. We can see the apple,
with the bite missing, in his hand.

But what is this falling like rain?
There are no clouds. Is it tears, or juice
from the apple? We must find the child's head.
He may be hurt. He may need someone
to find his head. And where is the sun?
Let us look for the sun. There are evidences
of it lighting the wings of birds. Somewhere
there must be a sun, and a child's head
with a bite of apple in its mouth.

ROBERTA SPEAR

Tom Peck

Born Sept. 26, 1948 in Hanford, California. The thing I remember most vividly about childhood were my dreams (about witches).

Went to school in Hanford, San Francisco, Santa Barbara, & Visalia. Spent third year of college at Irvine (Univ. of Calif.) where I befriended poet Galway Kinnell, an association that has probably had the most impact on my writing to date. Spent summer of '69 in Sheffield, Vermont (8 miles from nowhere) with he, his wife, and two children on their farm. While there I came to realize that things like the sprouting of the garden's first head of lettuce, the chickens laying their first eggs, and the raccoon eating one of the chickens, become the most important events in daily life; and when the trees stop calling you by name, you know that you're in the right place.

Returned to California and entered Fresno State College, where I am currently studying under, and receiving immeasurable help from, poet Phil Levine. I know I'll eventually end up in the mountains again though.

I don't always fully understand my poems myself immediately after they've been written. I usually write while feeling desperate or exhilarated, and often find myself transferring those emotions into my work, especially when overwhelmed by the pure physicalness of myself, other people, or my surroundings, and when my senses and ability to express myself verbally become inadequate. Because I am a visual poet and tend to write intuitively my poems often appear to follow a dream-like sequence and defy rationalization:—momentary flashes and spurts of energy with vague transitions.

I resent the common association between the woman poet and and neurosis, defeminization, and kitchen sinks. Because poetry should be the product of one's spirit, soul, unconscious, etc. it should not be categorized according to one's physical state, but rather that physical state should be used as a tool or an asset.

COMMON AFFAIR

1.

A brown candlestick holds up the kitchen table—
it is the only sign of help tonight.

I do not like you
rolling away—heavy smelling
of smoke and yellow ashes standing
erect too long;
of ingrown dust; dusty hands
skimming their sweat across the table
instead, shaking the particles off
at the moon:

2.

Its light has slipped from a slender waist
but the lap, still spread with a napkin, is ready.
Like my pilgrim skirt, it shuffles

and then stops to eat the natives.

There is no one here to pull it up,
to weave the drawstrings in and out
of the skeleton bones. There is no one here
to wear it:

the moon's light hangs as useless in this room
as your dead steer-tongue.

3.

A certain fear
hobbles up the back of my neck
and throbs in that skin turned white,
like the collar piece of a nun
as she lifts her palms upward
under the streetlight
and shakes the steel bars of each beam
between the shadows. The nun in me
screams:

"I am really a stoic;
my head is resting on your belly;
I go to bed for forty days
and nights in the same t-shirt hanging
to my thighs. I was never the kind of child
to get up and ask for a drink of water."

4.

Judas stands in the corridor—tight-lipped,
unflinching;
Judas shoves the crumbs under the table;
Judas smiles at the reflection of his smile
in limping eyes, in
the moon waiting;
Judas wrings his hands for more bread; eats
and wrings;
Judas buckles in at the groin.

5.

The footsteps of the moon have become so loud
that it sounds like someone
is walking behind it:

the tongue retreats,
the steel bars of white teeth crack,
the moon leaves, the moon
is a stone-deaf woman.

Judas, I will be your nurse
if you will roll over and look up at me.
If you will cough I will be her.

Judas if you were a black man,
as black as this night,
you would still be Judas.

6.

I peel the sticky lids apart
and suck on the brine; I
rise—

place the candle by my bed, close
to my cheek:
even its soft and naked hairs
will not jump out at you, they too
are shy. Stroke them,
stroke them.

ON THE PIANO

My grandmother's fingers
touch the music of their bones:

a sound breaks in the brittle skin;
the heart and life lines rock
sending ripples of sweat to the surface,
like air rising from the foam of a sinking wave;

rings on a tree trunk are blown away;
the lines fall, as sickles
to the handful of roots.

The bones answer back, like a bird
calling "Burned,
burned" from a frozen nest,
and slide from the whiteness of that shadow,
from the clear ashes batted around in the air
over a village. The bones float down
on the backs of stone-colored moths, confused
by their own separation.

By their separate knowledge,
the gnarled faced children
climb out of the windows and leave
the burning houses.

The hot eyes look upward
to the sky—the birds call:

the noise of a screw being turned
into a hole—
an uncontrolled ear;
the shuffle of chairs and beds melting
away from our bodies and moving out
on a current of smoke, or the extra skin
of fingers slipping into a crack
between two keys on the piano.

FIRST PLANTING

1.

I can't forget
that these are only people growing
in my garden
whose arms rise
and fight, like tongues
leaving the mouth, for affection;

whose knuckles turn white
trying to shovel dirt over
my feet, thinking
that I will go with them:
but they always end by beating themselves
back into the ground—

They are only petals split in half
by a beak falling through the air.

I dance in the field
with my pant legs rolled and boots
the same color as my eyes
kick through the dust collected
on their lips,
knocking the metal pins
from their jaws. I watch them
breathe:

2.

The sound of a shovel
hitting the ground
is one sound; it continues
because it wants to—
They make a slit from my collar
to my waist and find:

a buried bag of petals and dirt
softly caked on roots
like a glove worn by softer bones;
a hoe and shovel
packed away in the sawdust
of sunken arteries;
a bottle left half-ful
with its own, murky water;

they find my stomach—
an empty cell where the kneeling prisoner
is drawn through the floor
into the ceiling of another cell;
and that lowest animal
feeling metal on a nerve, screaming
up to them.